BOB BREEN

sparring

STRATEGY · TACTICS · TECHNIQUE

For Terry and Maria

The martial arts are by their very nature physically challenging and anyone training for the first time should consult a medical practitioner. Martial Arts training should only be undertaken by students who are supervised by a qualified teacher, holding specialist insurance, who is sanctioned by a recognised governing body. Whilst every effort has been made to ensure that the advice, principles, concepts and techniques presented in this book are technically accurate, neither the author nor the publisher can accept responsibility for any damage, injury or loss sustained as a result of the use of this material.

© 2009, Bob Breen
Photography by Pete Drinkell
Edited by Jamie Hutchins
Designed by Stephanie de Howes
First Edition

Published by the Bob Breen Academy
16 Hoxton Square, London N1 6NT
T: 020 7729 5789
E: enquiries@bobbreen.co.uk
www.bobbreen.com

ISBN 978-0-9560753-0-7

Printed and bound in Great Britain

Contents

CHAPTER I What is sparring?

Sparring is a form of practise fighting. Throughout the history of combat, fighters have sought ways to make the frenzied and chaotic unknown of combat controllable, and outcomes more predictable. By using a mix of drilling, conditioning and sparring methods, combatants can achieve more predictable results. This book aims to improve your fighting chances: you will understand different sparring methods, their supporting techniques, and learn to break down your sparring practise into manageable chunks. This knowledge will transform your sparring.

What is sparring

Various martial art systems define sparring in different ways. Some systems use the term 'sparring' in a generic sense to describe many of their two-person drills. These are often fixed drills, employing simple attacks with the hands or legs, in one-step or three-step variations. In these drills, the defensive technique is applied against the attack which comes on the first or third step. These can be a simple, effective way to start, but this approach doesn't teach flow and doesn't translate to free sparring, which is the focus of this book.

In free sparring you can use any technique you want, at any time. Free sparring is a practise fighting method that encompasses much of the randomness and freedom common to real fighting. In an attempt to give you a body of skills to work with, most systems use a number of preset drills as a foundation. In sparring though, these preset drills and skills can be hard to remember. You need a progressive training programme that, though it starts with drilling basics, goes on to bridge the gap between drilling and sparring. Ultimately, it means you can employ the necessary skills and techniques without conscious thought. I'll cover a number of methods you can employ, so that you get better at subconsciously employing skills when the right opportunity presents itself.

To get good at free fighting, whatever the format, you just have to do it. No drill allows you to practise the broken beat and syncopated timing of real sparring. Most drills, out of necessity, are on the beat and rhythmic in nature. Free sparring, by contrast, has an unfixed rhythm: sometimes it has a stammer-like gap between blows, at other times a constant and intense interchange. Sparring, like real fighting, doesn't just happen on a forwards-and-backwards axis but spirals and turns, and it's hard to develop training methods that replicate this. What I've tried to do in this book is to break sparring down into bite-sized chunks to give you sparring scenarios, training methods and drills that focus on one essential part at a time. They will give you a way to understand the landscape of each particular scenario and familiarize you with the shapes that present themselves.

'A rice pounder becomes a rice pounder when he pounds rice'

I'll start by talking about tools and establishing contact levels. Sparring must be organised to suit your level of ability, it is a gradual process and you need to start at the beginning. Sometimes sparring can be very light and playful, and at other times it can be as hard as real fighting (although normally it lacks the venom and emotional intensity of a real fight). The amount you do of each sort, both playful and hard, is important. At one time, my club focused mainly on hard sparring. We got good at fighting to an extent, but I only had a few students. No-one wanted to take any chances because of how hard we hit and we didn't grow. It was always an exercise in machismo with little benefit. Now, I use lots of easy sparring with the occasional hard, pressured bout. As a result my school has grown and my students have become harder and more accomplished fighters.

Many students don't arrive with any experience of fighting and are not sure if they are tough enough for the challenge of sparring. I tell them not to worry about their toughness or resilience. You don't notice yourself getting tougher – it comes in small improvements over time. I often advise them that it's like gold leaf; each leaf itself isn't thick but put them together over time and you've got a gold bar. Any person can learn to spar and become very good at it, given the right training and coaching. The extra percentage that the great fighters have is down to natural talent. However, if they aren't training and sparring, and you are, many of the advantages that their talent affords are cancelled out.

It's important that sparring isn't too traumatic for you. If it is, you won't do more of it, and above all that's what you have to do. What you'll find is that some days you'll do really well and be full of your own ability, but others you will find it challenging and even depressing. Your ability to put up with this flux is what makes you a great fighter. It's about building experience: as Bruce Lee advised, 'research your own experience.' Obviously, the more experience you've got the more you have to work with. Hard or soft, it's all movement and interplay between you and your opponent.

A variety of sparring partners at different levels, both above and below yourself, is also good to have. Regardless of whether your opponent is more or less skilled, you get different but equally useful insights.

Filipino martial arts teachers often use a triangle to symbolise the reality of fighting. One side of the triangle is technique, the second courage, and the third luck. You can work hard to improve technique and can build courage through familiarity of what may seem a chaotic and traumatic scenario. Luck is luck, although the more training and preparation you do the luckier you will find you become.

So what exactly is sparring? This book is focused on a boxing, kickboxing and mixed martial arts approach. Throwing, grappling and clinch methods are out of the scope of this book, but are nonetheless crucial elements of fighting. If you train in a more traditional method like Karate or Taekwondo, the basics of striking and kicking are very similar. It doesn't matter whether it's called a right cross or a gyakuzuki, kicks and punches from all styles share essentially the same characteristics. Similarly, the basics of strategy are the same. You'll find lots of tips throughout the book to make you more successful, regardless of your training background and preferred style.

The fighter's toolbox presented here will contain the standard punches from boxing, plus some of the kicks used in kickboxing or Thai boxing (described later in the next chapter). I haven't been too specific about how you perform these in this book as detailed technical instruction can be found in my book *Fighting – A path to understanding* (see Resources). As a starting point, if your punch or kick hits the target you're doing it right; if you're not, it's wrong. You can of course go back and refine each tool *ad infinitum* because you can always tweak it to get more power, to reduce preparation, or to make it less visible to your opponent. Constant improvement is a lifetime's work. "Drill-spar-drill-refine-drill-spar-drill-refine" is the mantra here, success is in your hands.

Once you understand the basic principles of sparring you can adapt them to fit whatever you want to do, whether that's throwing elbows, using takedowns or anything else. This book simply shares a basic, progressive programme, with ideas on how to overcome common problems that nearly everyone comes up against as they develop their skills.

It's important, if you are just starting out, to understand what sparring is. My own first experience of sparring wasn't particularly great. I knew a bit about real 'street' fighting as I'd done quite a lot, but after a year of formal training I was a true Karate believer. My instructor said, 'tonight we're going to do sparring,' so I went into my deep stance as soon as we started. I promptly got kicked in the groin by my training partner with a full-power rear leg front kick. Ouch! Well if that doesn't put you off, what will? It's important to realise that it's fighting, not quite real fighting, but close enough. As boxing referees say, 'protect yourself at all times.' Regardless of whether you have a good instructor or are training yourself, it's important early on to delineate the boundaries of what is allowed and expected, and then work out from there. Think of it like a jigsaw. Work out from the top corner and do the easy edges, and then fill in the complex bits at your leisure.

Go slow and grow.

CHAPTER 2 Laying the groundwork

Let's get started by putting down some basic kicking and punching tools so that we have an established framework. Then you can adapt this to suit your style of fighting. We'll then set down some ground rules about contact levels and pace that will keep you safe. Start slow and safe and build confidence at first. Eventually you can go as hard as you like, by then you'll have a cool head that can deal with any pressure.

Equipment

So what equipment are you going to need? We'll cover lots of different types of training in this book so we'll need a couple of types of glove and some body protection.

Some people don't like wearing lots of body protection, whereas others like lots. The aim of protective equipment isn't to act as a form of armour, it's so that you can spend more time sparring with less downtime due to injuries such as bruised shins. Personally, I rarely wear a groin box and feel better without one. However, I probably got more kicks in the groin from training partners over the years, but I also learnt how to stay up and control pain. Start with the level of protection that makes you feel safe, then occasionally fight without it so that you experience the fear of not having your usual kit. The control is taken away from you and it makes you mentally stronger. Just remember the aim is to do lots of sparring and enjoy the process.

> 14oz Boxing gloves

> Padded bag gloves or 8/10oz gloves

> Gumshield

> Shin and instep guards

> Groin box

IMPORTANT

Your best protection comes from good technical fighting skills plus good foot-work and body placement to keep you out of trouble. We'll cover each of these in the following chapters.

Tools

Overleaf is a list, in photographic form, of the punches and kicks that we'll use in this book. It's not my intention to go into too much depth on how to perform these here. I've assumed a basic level of competence and that you know these techniques. If not, come back to this book once you've learned them from your instructor or my previous book.

Do you need all of these techniques straight away? No, you can start sparring with just the jab, cross and hook, then add the front and round kick. Bring in new techniques as you learn them. As you'll see later, when it comes to sparring sometimes less can be more. If you're from a traditional style, adapt the techniques that you have been taught to the methods in this book. We've all only got two arms and two legs, so although there are lots of variations between styles, to paraphrase Bruce Lee, 'a punch is a punch and a kick is a kick'. If there's a method that you know from your previous training that isn't covered here, put it into your sparring. That's why it's called 'free sparring'. The only rule is to take care of your training partners whilst, paradoxically enough, trying to hit them.

2.1 > JAB, a) front view, b) side view

a)

b)

2.2 > STRAIGHT RIGHT, a) front view, b) side view

a)

b)

2.3 > LEFT HOOK

2.4 > LEFT OPEN HAND SLAP

2.5 > RIGHT HOOK

2.6 > RIGHT OVERHAND

2.7 > RIGHT SHOVEL HOOK

2.8 > LEFT SHOVEL HOOK

2.9 > RIGHT UPPERCUT

2.10 > LEFT UPPERCUT

2.11 > STRAIGHT BLAST / CHAIN PUNCH, a) left then, b) right hand

a)   b)

2.12 > REAR LEG FRONT KICK, a) knee chambered, b) full extension

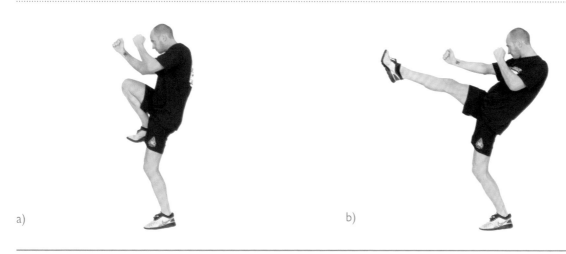

a)   b)

2.13 > LEAD LEG FRONT KICK, a) knee chambered, b) full extension

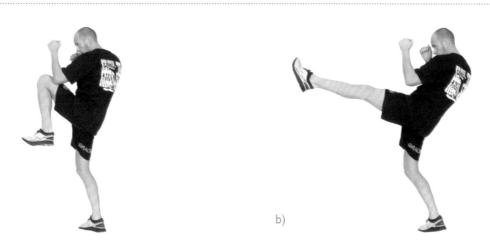

a)   b)

2.14 > SNAP ROUND KICK, a) leg chambered, b) full extension

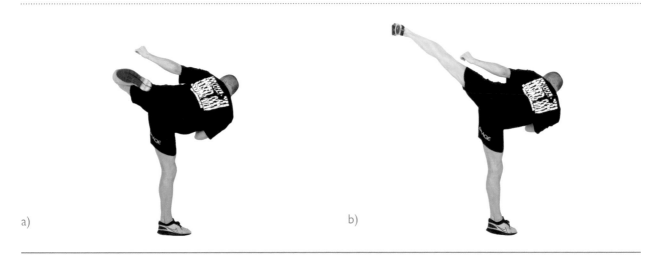

a)   b)

2.15 > HIGH ROUND KICK

a)   b)   c)

2.16 > BACK KICK, a) turn and chamber leg, b) full extension

a)   b)

2.18 > OBLIQUE KICK

2.19 > LONG KNEE

2.20 > SIDE KICK

If you don't want to use the tools that I've listed here because you think that your own system or styles are better, go ahead – it's not that important. Just choose a few of the high percentage techniques, and any that are similar to those

I've outlined, and start from there. To become a 'well-rounded' fighter you're going to have to understand the whole game and train within various parameters, against every type of attack. Wherever you start, you'll get to everything in time.

Contact levels

The majority of people don't have a death wish or a deep masochistic bent. They just want to get better at fighting. There are many reasons why people want to be able to fight: for some it's a way of dealing with a fear of confrontation and conflict, for others it's a way of proving themselves and gaining confidence. It can be a sort of rite of passage. Therefore it's important to set up some sort of agreed contact level when starting to spar. I use two methods in my own club to get people started and to acclimatise them to contact – static tapping and moving tapping.

STATIC TAPPING

I get each of the participants, in turn, to tap one another on the forehead whilst looking at each other until they come to an agreed level of force. This level is normally not high, but it's still contact, and not totally under your control, so it's a great place to start. Your confidence goes up because you think, 'oh, I can handle that'. Then you are off and running. The contact level may escalate during the sparring session, but you should try not to go too far from the established working zone.

MOVING TAPPING

This is a means of improving your slipping and evasion skills. Your opponent taps you on the head with both left and right punches. Not hard punches. If it's too hard, let him know and agree a level you can work with. Focus on keeping your eyes open with a strong gaze. Once you can do this, you move towards him whilst still being hit, keeping your head forwards. Once you've proved your resilience and fortitude to yourself, and gained control over your fear of contact, you can start to slip and bob and weave so that you don't get hit as much. Some strikes will still get you, but you've dealt with that earlier when you were a passive target, like a nail, so you can deal with it again. Now you're somewhere between being a hammer and a nail. Don't fall foul of peer group pressure and bang too hard – just challenge your opponent enough to make their eyes close. Only strike to the forehead.

Control

If you are going to spar, it's important that there is a third person there to control things. Often emotions come to the fore and you can find yourself lashing out. You end up scrapping, not sparring, and not in control of yourself. You want to be like a professional and keep your ego in control. A third party can intercede, can keep heads cool and can keep you focused on the skills or aspects of fighting that you are trying to master.

The worst training partners are those who vary their contact level. These are the type of people who tell you they want to go easy, then, when an opportunity presents itself, let you have the best shot that they've got. These 'cheap shots' should be avoided when you find them. Some of these people are scared at their core and do anything to get an advantage, not realizing that keeping steady under fire is what it's all about. Don't let this be you! Be dependable, be steady and take care of your training partners. You'll have more people to train with and you'll therefore get more experience.

Other people might appear to be trying to beat you up, but in fact they are just heavy handed. As long as they're constant then at least you know what you're getting into, and you can protect yourself at all times. If your school or club is the right type of environment you should be able to talk to them about your concerns regarding contact levels or ask them for help on a particular area. After all, a person like this also needs training partners of all levels to improve themselves. As he helps you, he will be helping himself.

The instructor or third party shouldn't let hot fights go on too long, and should use their judgement here. Make people shake hands or pay respects at the beginning and end of sparring. This keeps heads cool and focused on the job in hand. Sometimes, rotating partners when one fight is getting heavy-handed defuses the situation. If someone is coming from a hard fight and going to a lower level student or beginner, the instructor can give them a coaching role or re-establish contact levels with the head-tapping drills we started this section with. The rule is that everyone grows and gets better – not only in their sparring but also in how they conduct themselves as a person, as a human being. 'Self-protection and then self-perfection,' as the saying goes, being a 'bad ass' fighter doesn't guarantee that you'll go very far in the world.

THE TALK TEST

A good way to ensure easy sparring is to apply the talk test. If you can still talk in meaningful sentences then the contact level is about right. If you can hardly breathe and can't even say your own name then the chances are that you are sparring at too high a level. Early on, most of your sparring wants to be at some sort of 'talk test' level. Even though you can speak, be careful, as an open mouth weakens the structure your jaw and will be a problem if you are hit. Once again, it's a place to start and to come back to, and re-assess contact or work-rate levels.

'Self-protection and then self-perfection'

Conditioning

Many people say that the three rules of fighting are conditioning, conditioning and conditioning. It's essential that before getting into sparring you have a good general fitness level. It's not my intention here to cover the area of conditioning in any depth. I'll just outline the areas that you should have under your belt or be working on.

You need to focus on the three core attributes – strength, stamina, and suppleness. First, work on your stamina and cardiovascular fitness. This can be radically improved by running, swimming or cycling. Stamina work needs to be regular but not every day, make it intermittent but challenging. Remember, improvements come in the recovery period. If you are unfit, then first establish a base level. Changes in tendon strength don't happen overnight so don't try going from zero to hero in one week – you'll only get injured. As soon as you can, bring in some sprints or gentle unstructured interval work whilst out on a run or bike ride. For instance, sprint between every third lamp-post, or to the stop sign at the end of the road. This doesn't have to be too structured, unless you're operating at the highest level, but make sure that you challenge yourself and your ability to change pace during your workouts. With cardiovascular training, work which challenges your body two or three times per week is better than going out and meandering at a constant pace every day. Don't over-train, either. Challenging workouts two or three times per week, done properly, are enough to improve your stamina for sparring.

Take the same approach with strength work. First, use body weight exercises to build strength in joints and tendons. These exercises build functional strength, that you need for fighting. There's a debate about the efficacy of body weight training versus weight training using dumbbells, bars and static machines. The latter can be a viable part of your programme but I prefer body weight exercises, with some weight training done in the winter to build core strength. Remember, you don't have to be big. I see lots of people who come into the club who have big muscles yet can't hit hard. Big leg muscles are great as a target for kicking, too, so just keep focused on the job at hand, which is to be good at sparring. If you find that you're being overpowered by opponents who have the same build as you, re-evaluate and bring in some focused resistance training. However, the place to start is with your own body, moving it around on

the ground can be very demanding. In addition, look at building core strength as this has a marked impact on striking skills. With good core conditioning your body moves as a unit and develops your ability to punch or kick above your weight. My recommendation is to first start with body weight exercises like push-ups, chins, squats, lunges, and cat licks to get started. There's a huge amount you can do here and then decide if you have a weak area that needs focused weight training or core stability training. There are numerous books out there on conditioning and I recommend Ian Oliver's **Boxing Fitness**.

Suppleness is good for both sparring and life! It should be a part of your daily routine. Exercises like the Yoga 'salute to the sun' in any of its varied forms are a great way to start. Many people only stretch certain muscles but you need to stretch head to toe to get the best effect. Look at stretching all of your muscle groups with attention paid to your core body, using twists and bends in addition to the basic leg and arm stretches. Good body mobility can get you out of trouble when sparring, and stretching is the place to start.

You also have to fit all of this into your life. If your schedule is tight, fit stretching in throughout your day when the opportunity arises. Body weight exercises can be fitted in more easily than going to the gym to lift weights. Do little bits throughout your busy life and you'll be amazed at the change. I remember setting up a chin bar in my bedroom doorway and would do five or ten whenever I went into the bedroom. Pretty soon I was doing well over a hundred chins per day with the corresponding benefit to my body. As self-help author Stephen Covey says in his books 'by the inch it's a cinch; by the yard it's hard.' (**The 7 habits of highly effective people**). Small steps with good quality recovery and no over-training are what you need. Remember: this is a long-term plan and becoming a great fighter takes years, not months. Consistency is the watchword here.

CHAPTER 3 Getting started

Here we're going to jump in and get started. Starting simply and then building in more complex strikes and variations. It's important to realise that even though we're covering simple skills that many may think are solely for the beginner these are also the most advanced skills too. It's about building experience and deep knowledge of the skills. Whatever your level this is a good chapter for you.

Range and measure

Fighting can be arranged into various spatial ranges – long, medium and short – as a way of making it more understandable. In reality it doesn't always fit into these neat categories but it's a good place for you to start learning. At long range, you can use your lead kicks and your rear kicks and sometimes the lead hand strikes. At medium range, you can use abbreviated or short kicks and most of your hand techniques. At close range, you can grapple, kick and knee, use punches like the uppercut and the hook, and other tools such as the

elbow. The best place to start to understand 'measure' is with your long range hand tools. Then, add in the kicks and other techniques to progressively build your understanding.

Taking the measure of someone, just as it sounds, involves building an appreciation of the measurement between your tools and those of your opponent. It involves knowing when you are in and out of range, and how to make the most of your measure by using good footwork and effective placement of your strikes. See *Fighting*.

Out of distance sparring

This is like virtual sparring, as if you were fighting against a computer: you don't get hit. What do you need to do? Start moving around opposite your opponent, throwing any punches that you like. The only rule is you have to be at a distance where you can't hit each other's hands. In reality it often gets a bit closer than this, but this is the benchmark. Vary the pace – slow is a good place to start, as it's much easier to pick up shapes and the forms that occur in sparring when you have the time to notice them. You can also do this type of sparring at a fast pace to challenge your cardiovascular system. If you go fast and hard for a long time you really get into anaerobic debt, where your body has to function without oxygen. This can replicate real fighting.

Start by using any of the hand strikes that you know, trying to fit them in-between your opponent's blows, responding to their movement. You should also be using evasive techniques and angling, to get your hits to 'strike' your virtual target. It is important to concentrate on good footwork, good balance, and economy of motion. You can often tell a beginner because of the sound that their feet make as he flitters and flutters around, not sure of any position he finds himself in. Go steady and focus your tools on your opponent.

Imagine your hand tools, as if you had punched with both of them at the same time, making a sharp, narrow, skewed triangle, the point of which is always facing towards your opponent. Your hands, when held in the standard guard, fall in the middle of the sides of this triangle, with your shoulders, forming the rearwards points. Your body should be side-on so that one shoulder is forwards and the other back, so that you present a narrow profile. Once you've got the basic idea you can play with it.

Be both conventional and unconventional. Any wild excesses and dreams will be tempered when your opponent really hits you – then you'll be more conservative. Emulation is a good method to use with a mentor or a better fighter than you, someone who's better than you and who's going to help you grow. Copy and clone his movement. No matter how hard you try you'll never become him and lose your own identity, but you will pick up nuances and subtleties on a subliminal level. The difference between a good and a great fighter is subtle.

When I was a green belt in Karate and starting to spar I needed some inspiration. I initially chose two people to emulate whose style suited me. One was Ticky Donovan who became a most successful competitor and long-time

British Karate coach. He was a brown belt at that point, so not that much higher than me, but at that time one of the best fighters. I copied him for about six months when I was doing my first competitions. Did it help? I'm sure it did; I had a successful template to work from. The second person I copied was Hisaomi Fujii who was All Japan champion at that time. He was a great counter-puncher and that fitted with the type of fighting I liked to do. I had fast hands and was courageous (or stupid) enough to stand my ground or evade and counter-punch. Initially, I was a copy of these two men but within a couple of fights the 'me' part of this triumvirate was blossoming and coming to the fore. Over time I added influences from various masters and great fighters but only where it fitted with me. It's important for your development to have fighting heroes that you want to emulate. Subconsciously you take on parts of their fighting

style. One of my boxing trainers, Clarence Prince, had Sugar Ray Robinson as his hero, so like Robinson he had a great left hook. I trained with him and did lots of sparring (including out of distance sparring). As a result I developed a very potent left hook.

'It's better to emulate genius than to create mediocrity.'

Whatever your level, keep out of distance sparring as part of your workout. Use it either as a warm-up before real sparring, as a cardio workout, or as a non-risk area in which to try out your ideas before subjecting them to a reality test. If you don't have a partner use solo shadow boxing to replicate as much of the feel of out of distance as you can.

3.1 > OUT OF DISTANCE SPARRING, sequence shows that there is no touching and that the fighters are responding to each other's movements.

Isolation sparring

Your next step is isolation sparring. This can be done in some form at any level of difficulty – even a high-level fighter should do some form of isolation work in which his favourite tool is denied him. Let's begin with the method that I use at my academy with those just starting to spar. I teach different isolation sparring techniques based around two attacking tools: the jab and the lead round kick. Once you've got these skills grooved and know the basics of how these tools work, we move on to using them in playful sparring. Initially, this is not too hard, just light contact or tagging. We can start with a drill for the low round kick and with the head-tapping for the jab. What's important about these first two types of isolation sparring is that they teach range and measure.

ISOLATION ONE: LEAD ROUND KICK SPARRING

Let's drill the lead round kick. Use a pendulum step, where the head keeps comparatively still whilst the legs move like a pendulum underneath. This pendulum action is less telegraphed and makes it harder for your opponent to see it coming. The rear heel comes to the lead heel, and you snap the kick from the knee. Alternatively, you can swing the kick from the hip (more typical of the Thai style), to strike the inside of the leg, but it's easier for them to come back at you behind your kick if you miss. If you swing the kick, it also means you're not training your appreciation of distance and measure. Do this isolation drill in a kick-for-kick fashion. Initially, go slowly, focusing on the technique and then chasing each other so you have to get out of distance quickly. As you will see we're almost sparring already.

3.2 > LEAD ROUND KICK SPARRING, sequence shows partners alternating the kick-for-kick drill.

TARGET

Whilst you're practising, the target is the lead leg on the inside of the thigh. Think of it as shorthand for what would be in reality a kick to the groin (one of Bruce Lee's favourite techniques.)

SUPPORTING TECHNIQUES

There are a number of techniques you can use to defend against the lead round kick.

3.3 > LEAD LEG CRUSH, this is the quickest to do, but you can get hurt.

PROTECTION

Because of this groin focus, you should consider wearing a groin box for protection. Also shin pads are recommended as often you will clash shin.

3.4 > LEAD LEG RETREAT I , the target lead leg is pulled back out of range by moving the hips and shoulders (almost into an opposite stance). The retreating foot only makes light contact with the ground before you skip back at your opponent with your own kicks.

3.5 > LEAD LEG RETREAT 2, unlike 3.4, the lead leg is stepped back out of range but the hips and body remain in the normal stance, with all your tools ready to launch your counter-attack as soon as your bring the lead leg back.

3.6 > OBLIQUE KICK BLOCK, this needs good timing, but is a good way to block the low kick and put you in a position to deliver a reply low kick.

ISOLATION TWO: JAB SPARRING

Start with the head-tapping that was covered in Chapter 2. Tap your opponent's forehead with a loose hand. Your opponent should focus on keeping his eyes open, with a strong gaze. Remember, in all the drills that follow that the target is the forehead. You'll need a few defensive techniques before you start.

REAR PARRY

An understanding of the rear parry is essential in defending against the jab. There are three main types: the parry, the catch, and the scoop. Let's look at them all in detail, in the following photos.

Snap-back

In addition, we'll introduce the snap back, an evasive technique that, when used in combination with the various parries, is very effective.

3.7 > PARRY, use your fingers and wrist to deflect your opponent's jab as it comes at you. Don't grab it, move it to where you think it should be, or try to stop the power – just do enough to make it miss. The closer it shaves you, the better.

3.8 > CATCH, just like catching a baseball in a mitt, you catch the jab in the palm of your hand and absorb some of the power. If it's really powerful or going through your block then you have to retreat your legs or use snapback to slow its progress.

3.9 > SCOOP, scoop the jab from a) inside to b) outside using your fingers and wrist. Start closer to your opponent and divert the punch as it travels towards you. Use the snapback to make this work even more effective.

a)   b)

3.10 > SNAP BACK, a) your rear heel should be raised and the ankle tense, with the body leaning forwards towards your opponent (demonstrated by black vest), b) snap the heel towards the floor to take you out of distance, but don't let it touch. You should, with a bit of tinkering, be able to create about 24 inches of space between your head and your opponent's punch. To add further distance, move the rear foot backwards and then snap-back. It sometimes takes a bit of playing with to get this really down but it's invaluable in sparring.

a)

b)

JAB-CATCH DRILL

This three-count drill from Filipino Kali uses both the catch and the snap-back to good effect. Direct a jab at your opponent's head. He snaps back, catches the jab and replies with his own jab. In turn, you catch that jab as you snap back, and reply with your own jab. Practise this where you lead for five or ten repetitions, then switch. For another, slightly harder method, change leader every three moves.

3.11 > JAB CATCH DRILL, sequence starts with a) jab towards opponent's head, b) they snap back and catch, replying with their own jab, which you avoid and catch. To complete the sequence, the initiator returns final jab (not shown).

a)

b)

STANDING SNAP-BACK DRILL

Your opponent holds his arm out, like a jab, and you lean forwards to place your forehead on his fist. Then use snap-back to move in and out, replacing your head on his hand each time. This will help you to calculate the shift in distance that you can achieve and find your measure.

SLIPPING / BOBBING

As your opponent throws a punch at you, move your head either to the side or slightly forwards towards his armpit. Either way, the blow misses and you're in an attacking position.

Jab sparring

Now that you have practised some defensive drills, it's time to have a bout of jab sparring. The aim of the exercise is to learn about your range and measure, so don't go too hard or fast. Before you start, as always, pay your respects to your partner, or touch gloves. Spar using the jab only, double and multiple jabs where appropriate, for one or two minute rounds. Try to use the jab and good footwork as you move backwards as well as moving forwards to attack. Good fighters have an aggressive defence and make you pay for any territory you take. Fake, if possible, to draw his parry, then move in behind it. You'll be helping him as he'll learn not to over-block

3.12 > THE SLIP

Adding more tools

If you're progressing well at the basic level and are enjoying it, then let's expand the toolbox and gradually add new variables. The initial aim is to get to the point where you have a standard sparring template. Remember though, this is only a place to start. Your eventual aim is to be outside any standard template unless it suits you. As Sun Tsu says in his **The Art of War**, 'Mix the orthodox with the unconventional.'

SIMPLE VARIATIONS

Here are a couple of variations that expand your toolbox a little without moving too far from the initial format:

> Jab on the high and low line

> Oblique kick

3.13 > JAB HIGH AND LOW, a) jab to the head or, b) to the stomach, or both in combination (a-b or b-a). Draw your opponent's defence high with your first jab then drop your body (like going down in an elevator) and jab to his body. Alternatively, jab to the stomach but keep your hand close to him, come up within his defensive structure (like in an elevator) and deliver the second jab, powering from the legs. Be careful to manage your contact level when going from low to high, as the range makes it easy to hit very hard.

a)   b)

3.14 > OBLIQUE KICK a) use the oblique kick to set up, b) the lead round kick. It can be used as a tool on its own, attacking the opponent's shin after your jab to stall any counter-attack on their part. As we've seen before it can also be used as a stop kick against the opponent's lead round kick.

a)   b)

THREE-WAY MIX

Mix all of the following variations together in your sparring. Add them into either of the two isolation methods previously:

> Use the jab to open up the high line and then kick on the low line

> Kick low and then jab to the high line

> Use the low kick to stop the jab

> Use the oblique to stop the jab

> Punch high then low

Now you are on your way. At the moment, we're mainly focusing on long-range tools because they are the tools on which to build your foundation. They will cause your opponent real problems and there are only a limited number of ways of overcoming them. As a result you will be able to funnel him into an area where your next level of defence is trained, focused and ready and waiting.

GO SLOW

As we are now going to bring in more tools it's important to go at a pace where you'll be successful. It's OK to go fast within the long range isolation sparring, but as you're building a full range of tools then it's time to put the brakes on and spar slowly. Later, once you've got the skills down, you can speed up, but not yet. You need to do lots of slow sparring, go at 30-50% of your maximum speed. As you introduce new tools, do it at a pace at which you can make the techniques successful. Remember, the talk test and contact levels previously discussed. In this instance it's OK if your opponent can see your blow coming and defend against it, even counter-attacking you. Don't take it personally, just enjoy the interchange. It's much like tennis players warming up before a match, exchanging shots but not seeking to win. In a way, you've got to invest in loss. As you'll see, once you don't mind being hit it makes you, paradoxically, harder to hit. You'll know when you're ready to go a little harder.

CHAPTER 4 Basic templates

Now we're going to introduce more tools so that you have a basic boxing and kickboxing template to work from. As I said before, if you use other fundamental techniques in your particular style of fighting then bring them in. I'm just using the template concept as a way of making your study of sparring easier to understand by going with commonly used basic techniques.

Cross, hook, uppercut, shovel hook

Let's bring in some other major hand tools: the cross, the hook, the uppercut and shovel hook. As I've covered most of these in some depth in my previous book, **Fighting**, let's go straight into some loop drills that will allow you to practise the hand tools and defensive techniques.

THE CROSS

Mechanically, the rear hand is one of the most powerful tools. Therefore it's important to have good technical skills to defend against it before putting it into your sparring mix.

The rear hand punch can come directly at you (the straight right), slightly across your centreline (the cross) or looping in from the blind spot on your left side (the right hook). For simplicity's sake let's address these as one type of blow and group all the defences together. We'll just divide them into ones that are coming straight and others that are coming wide.

Much like the 'jab-catch' drill in the previous chapter, the following loop drills will allow you to repeat basic skills over and over again and hard-wire them into your body. Some of these defences work for all three types of blow and some only for one. Don't 'help' him by not aiming your punches at the target, if your partner is having problems, just go slower. In all these loop drills you start with a strike (in this case the cross, later the hook) which you aim at your opponent's chin. They then use any of the defences shown in the following sequence of photos. The defender the returns the same strike at you, and you in turn defend. You practise as a continual loop, with both individuals getting taking turns to attack and then defend.

4.1 > SHOULDER ROLL, start with the core of your defence, learn the shoulder roll against the straight right or cross.

4.2 > OUTSIDE PARRY, a) outside parry or, b) insertion, against the straight right.

a)

b)

4.3 > HIGH ELBOW, against the straight right or cross, your hand grabs the top of your head and your elbow 'destroys' the fist.

4.4 > LOW ELBOW, against the straight right or cross, your hand is supported against the ribs and your elbow 'destroys' the fist.

4.5 > FOREARM ROLL, a) starts as a bong sao against the cross, b) your fist pivots around your elbow, and c) a swings over your opponent's arm.

a)   b)   c)

4.6 > INSIDE SHIELD, against a wide cross or hook.

4.7 > BICEPS STOP, against all wide blows.

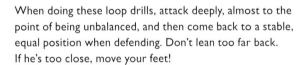

When doing these loop drills, attack deeply, almost to the point of being unbalanced, and then come back to a stable, equal position when defending. Don't lean too far back. If he's too close, move your feet!

Important: Use your lead hand as the arbiter of what is inside and what is outside. The more extended it is initially, the easier and earlier you'll be able to choose. Think of it as an early warning station.

The one defensive technique that doesn't fit into this neat loop drill is the 'bob and weave'. The bob and weave brings you up outside his arm where you are positioned best to hook. To bring it into a looping drill, try the following: 1) Your opponent throws the rear right hook, and you bob and weave underneath, 2) then he throws the left hook (or wide slap if you like) and you bob and weave under that (see, photo sequence 4.8 a-h, next page).

IMPORTANT
Use your lead hand as the arbiter of what is inside and what is outside. The more extended it is initially, the easier and earlier you'll be able to choose. Think of it as an early warning station.

4.8 > BOB AND WEAVE LOOP DRILL, you can bob and weave against most angles of blow, although it's much more difficult against a straight blow as you will need space and time to move into safety. a) to h) show bob and weave against right and left hooks. i) to l) show bob and weave with cross guard, against a possible knee attack.

Sparring: the rear hand

After practising the loop drills, go ahead and add the rear hand to your sparring mix. You can do it on its own as a single direct attack. Later, for an even more effective punch, you can hide it from your opponent until the moment it hits, using the jab to set up the cross. Aim the jab at his eyes and he won't be able to see the cross as it starts, which

challenges his defence. Think about using variable timing and variable levels of power with every blow. Do the jab powerfully a number of times to make him more reactive, they don't even have to hit the target but have to hit something, even the arms will often work. Then slide the cross in straight afterwards.

4.9 > LOOPING CROSS

4.10 > STRAIGHT RIGHT, penetrating.

4.11 > LOW KICK, against the cross.

4.12 > STOP HIT JAB (LEG), against cross.

4.13 > STOP HIT JAB (HAND), against cross.

Experiment with delivering the rear hand strike at different angles. Punch straight at first, then hook your blow around your opponent's lead hand. Then try a cross that slides through the gap where his arm is crooked in guard. You can throw the arm first and let the body follow, or use the body and let the arm follow. Both are OK; find out what works for you.

Which works for you? Remember the rule – if it hits it's good, if it doesn't it needs more work or isn't right for you at this time in your sparring development. Don't give up, later it may become your favourite move. Most techniques work if done in the right way. It's all about finding out what other things – timing, distance, and position – you have to change to move it from your 'could work' folder into your 'favourite tools' folder.

If you're defending, be careful when you circle to the left. Moving left leaves you with a big gap in your defence. When possible, move to the right; it makes it much harder for his cross to reach you. Occasionally move to the left, but only once you've retreated a little so the percentages are in your favour. Just be careful when moving in this direction.

The rear hand punch is a big move and novice fighters often use some sort of preparation; they 'telegraph' their move. This gives you the time to deal with it, move out of distance, pre-empt with your jab or front foot jab as they get set, or keep your distance and still hit him by striking with kicks. You can still use the lead low round kick if you do it early to attack his preparation. Even better, attack his lead leg with your rear round kick once his attack is ended and he's over-extended. Keep your guard up and keep it fluid with both hands being not only defences, but also potential weapons.

Sparring: the hook

If your opponent is coming towards you then the hook is the tool to use. It's not as long range as the punches in the cross family; think of it as closing the door on someone coming towards you. Sometimes you use it because you've missed with a jab or cross and he's now coming within the imaginary triangle you made by extending your hands together (previously discussed, Chapter 3). Sometimes he'll get inside your measure by slipping, by bobbing and weaving or perhaps just overwhelming you with an attack, the first part of which has missed. (It doesn't matter how close it came, don't worry about that – a miss is a miss.) Close the door with a shoulder roll and whipping the hook into the side of his head. You can hook without doing the defensive shoulder roll but you won't be hitting with your body behind the blow and your likelihood of getting hit increases. Here's a good drill for working on this approach to hooking. This is a variation that builds skills that can be used in what is sometimes called 'attack by drawing'.

CROSS-HOOK LOOP PAD DRILL

Get your training partner to hold the focus pads in a tight L-shape. Throw a cross at the pad in your partner's rear hand, then retreat your body by transferring your weight from the lead towards the rear and simultaneously deliver a hook onto the other pad. Keep it tight so that you can't wind up the arm. Instead, use the twist of your body and the built-up tension in the chest to power the blow. Like all loop drills, you make the best use of your time with no pre-amble or ritual at the end of each technique. It more closely resembles sparring and puts it into your bones.

You may initially find it hard to add the hook to your sparring mix. Often, beginners chase retreating opponents and try to hook but end up slapping. Not that this is necessarily bad, if you lead hook, as it can set up the cross or the rear kick. To get the hook to work defensively takes a good sense of timing. Doing the drill above is an essential way for you to learn the required timing and get a feel for when the opportunity might strike. Use a forwards hook if your opponent doesn't come in. If your opponent stands his ground, you can work on hitting to the body and then the head or double up on the high hook so that you use it twice. Remember, close the door to your chin by turning your body and keeping the lead shoulder raised.

UPPERCUT AND SHOVEL HOOK

Use the uppercut and shovel hook as attacks at close quarter or as your next line of defence, if he's got past your long range tools. They can be integrated into your combinations in attack and defence. Don't try to do these at long distance, they don't work there. Instead, use the jab and cross at long range, and the uppercut and shovel hook when your opponent is closer. That said, the shovel hook can be used at a greater distance than the uppercut.

These punches work best when you've moved or slipped to the left or right against your opponent. Alternatively, use them when he slips your jab or cross, when the spatial relationship is the same as if you had slipped or moved to the side. Following are a number of simple ways that you can use these punches both defensively and in attack.

4.14 > UPPERCUT, a) opponent slips outside your jab, b) you rear uppercut to their chin.

a)   b)

4.15 > UPPERCUT, a) opponent slips inside your jab, b) you rear uppercut to their chin.

a)   b)

4.16 > a) STEP or SLIP LEFT and b) UPPERCUT up the middle.

a)   b)

4.17 > UPPERCUT TO COMBINATION, a) opponent slips outside your cross, b) you lead uppercut, follow-up with c) rear cross, d) lead hook in combination.

a)

b)

c)

d)

4.18 > FLURRY OF UPPERCUTS, a) to c) use a flurry of uppercuts – they need not be powerful – to lift opponent's head, d) finish with lead hook. Do this to a crouching opponent who's attacking your body, or bobbing and weaving.

a)

b)

c)

d)

Sparring: adding kicks

Now we've got a hand-based sparring mix with a couple of easy-to-use low kicks. Let's expand the kick repertoire with front, round and side kicks.

The first technique to add is the rear round kick to the thigh. Aim at a target about six inches above the knee. Do this gently with each other as an initial drill. This kick attacks his base and extended lead leg, thus reducing his ability to carry out risk-free strong hand attacks. Keep the leg straight, but let it fold slightly upon contact if you don't want to hurt your opponent. Once you've got this down then bring your attack up to rib level or, if you are flexible enough, to head level.

Once you've started you need to be working on a number of things. Make sure that you have your hands arranged in a good defensive structure as you kick. Your hands should transition as you kick, in the following order – lead hand covers, rear arm crush (or define the line) and then return to left hand cover. Add angling to your mix so that you're not directly in front of your opponent.

This all sounds simple but many senior fighters don't have good skills here and as a result take more punishment than they need. Not too hard initially; remember they have to be able to walk out of training.

LEAD ROUND KICK (version two)

Now add in the lead round kick, initially to the inside of the leg. Try to do this without a preparatory step, instead, use a hip twist and rotate in the direction of the kick. Twist on your rear foot so the foot points backwards and swing the lead leg whilst keeping it straight. Dropping your stance extends the range of the kick. Target the inside leg, behind the muscle on top of the knee. This kick is different from the earlier lead round kick which we covered. That one was delivered with a flick and would, in a real fight, be aimed at the groin. It is great for learning distance and measure. This one, however, is to attack and 'destroy' his lead leg. Once you're comfortable at this height then you can hit targets higher up the body. If you're trying to hit higher targets, stomp with your right leg and use the power it provides to drive your lead leg upwards. Other alternatives are to do a replacement step, to briefly bring your lead leg to the rear, or a step to the right. Do these on their own until you have them well-practised before adding them to your sparring mix.

4.19 > STEP AND ROUND KICK, notice defensive structure of hands, follow kick with hand combination.

4.20 > a) STOMP REAR LEG, and b) LEAD MIDDLE KICK

....

a)   b)

4.21 > REPLACEMENT STEP AND ROUND KICK, a-c), also called a switch-kick.

....

a)   c)

KICK FOR KICK

In this drill you take it in turn to kick and alternate legs. One person kicks and the other one circles or curves away from it, at the same time preparing for his own attack. This is important: think of starting your attack, or at least getting your stance and balance in place, during their attack. You can attack high or low and with either leg. Keep your hands up – initially don't do anything with them, but after a little while you can gently wrestle or look for open lines with the hands.

Don't focus too much on the hands: what you want to get is the angling and position. Don't take big steps to the left or right as this will leave your leg exposed and weak – an ideal target. Take small steps only. If his kick is strong, don't go hard and rigid like a rock, rather, let the energy be absorbed into your movement. It hurts less. Kick for kick is a great drill and in reality you're sparring, back and forwards, with only one kick at a time. Once you've got this down then do two kicks for two kicks. Later you can add different types of kick like the front kick or long knee. It's the concept that matters, though this concept works best with the round kick.

4.22 > KICK FOR KICK, shown as a sequence.

FRONT KICK

Front kicks can be hard to deal with as they penetrate deeply. However, you can often divert them with your elbows or crush them with your raised leg. Alternatively, if the preparation is obvious, you can stop-hit them or move away. It's the unseen front kick that is the big danger. Make this your kick. Fake the jab high, to draw the eyes up, and then slide the front kick in below. The greater the distance between these two blows, the harder it is for your opponent to handle.

The lead leg short foot jab is a great way to set up a following one-two with the hands. This differs from a penetrating front kick as it has less drive through the target. In both instances, make sure your hips are raised, with

your supporting leg straight. For best results, use the short foot jab defensively and make it sharp. It's very simple and effective but hard to make the most of unless you train it hard. If the distance to your target is too great, it is important to hide any preparation, as this will act as a signal to your opponent and allow them to defend or counter. The best method of covering ground is to hop in behind any type of front kick ensuring that your body weight is behind your kick when you make contact. If you need to step in rather than hop, it's important that you cover your step with some sort of hand blow or feint, to act as a distraction and gets their body weight or head moving backwards so it is hard to set up a counter.

4.23 > FRONT KICK BLOCKED BY RAISED KNEE

4.24 > FRONT KICK DIVERTED BY ELBOW, notice shift in body structure also.

4.25 > a) FAKE HIGH JAB, and b) LOW FRONT KICK

a)

b)

SIDE KICK

The side kick works best when you are sparring at long range. Fake high and then come in to attack the ribs with the kick. Alternatively, you can use it with a spin which is highly effective. As both methods are direct, on a straight trajectory, it's hard for an opponent to deal with. Although due to the long distance involved it is easier if you don't fake the high line well enough. The spinning side kick can be used when he comes towards you and you appear to retreat or shoulder roll, continue the motion around into the kick. Alternatively, when your front or round kicks haven't connected and leave you in a weakened position that is going to be attacked, you can use the spinning side kick to recover the offensive.

We've now got a standard template to work from. To this you can add whichever other kicks you know. Add them one at a time, or, if you feel like it, dump them all into the mix at the same time! The aim is to just get you sparring. Start with low kicks, but as soon as your ability develops, do them to all heights. Starting to free-spar is quite a big step, especially if you are throwing everything into the mix at once. Remember, you can always go back a bit and just use isolation sparring on each of the tools in turn. Alternatively, adopt a simplified structure like sparring with the jab and cross only then adding in more tools, one at a time. Don't hurry to be an expert. In truth, even the most experienced fighter should go back and do isolation sparring in some form every week. You should always enter sparring with a game plan and something that you wish to work on and improve.

4.26 > SIDE KICKS, a-c) practised in kick for kick format, at different heights.

a)

b)

c)

Timing and rounds

By now you should be expanding the time you're sparring to three-minute rounds. This is an arbitrary measure, most commonly used in boxing matches. It may not sound much but three minutes will tax your cardiovascular system enough, and you should allow a half-minute or minute recovery period between rounds. As part of your training, make sure to train over-time and under-time. Do rounds, on the bag or pads, that are four or five minutes long so you build up your endurance and then do shorter rounds so that you know about intensity. Lie to your training partners, tell them they are only going to do one or two minutes and they should go all out, but then make them go a minute longer. This idea, which should only be used occasionally, is important as in a fight you'll often be forced to go past the point where you expected to go to. The ability to dig in and endure is part of making you a great fighter. As I've said before, spar slowly to get technical skills down. Go faster when you feel you can't do the slow stuff any more. However the slow stuff is where you'll improve your game.

Combinations

Following are examples of common mini-combinations, using the skills we've outlined. They are simple, yet work well in sparring. Train them on your own in shadow boxing or in partner drills. Don't take on too many as you won't remember them in sparring. It's better to own one and be working on another, than to have five that you can't use. Once you've got each down on a physical level then start sparring them. I often say in the classes that I teach that if you just practise the technique in the class or training session the technique is still mine. It's like borrowing from a library – it's just on loan. Use it outside, however, and it's yours forever. Don't loan it – own it! Play with the timing and power variables. Once you've got them down, leverage your ability by working through the next chapter on position so that it makes it harder for your opponent to counter.

'Know five, own three, master one'
BOB BREEN

4.27 > a) LOW JAB, b) leading to a HIGH LEAD HOOK

a)

b)

4.28 > a) FOOT JAB, b) JAB, c) CROSS, thrown in combination.

4.29 > JAB, JAB, CROSS, thrown in combination.

RELAX

Often at this point in sparring, beginners are very tense in the top of their body. Relax. Think of dropping your body focus downwards towards your navel and breathing lower down, if possible. Imagine what it feels like to be a pro-fighter. How would you move? More smoothly, languidly with that ease where they don't seem to move fast but arrive quickly. Imagine this and bring it into your body feel.

TIP: Who are you?

Only you know about your weaknesses, be they psychological or physical. Your opponent only knows what you show him. I often ask under-confident students to imagine how they would feel if they had just come back from two tours in the SAS or SEALS or were hardened ring veterans from numerous Thai boxing matches around the world. What would you feel like? IMAGINE THAT MENTAL ATTITUDE: 'Impervious to blows,' 'been there done that,' 'no problem, I like it when it's tough.' Imagine this and bring it into your body structure. Imagination is a huge tool. Fantasise, meditate, imagine – whatever works for you, but show yourself what you are capable of in your imagination and then do it for real, now, in today's sparring. It's attitude we're working on here.

CHAPTER 5 Position

They say the three laws of business success are: location, location, and location. Similarly, where you are in relation to your opponent makes a huge difference to your fighting success. You need to understand angles and distance. The place where your opponent is attacking is where you should not be. Failing that, you should be in a position that restricts his options. There are a number of approaches presented here that will make you harder to hit. First, let's deal with an understanding of angles and measure. I'll start by showing you the safety zones when using hand techniques, and then we'll go onto look at zero pressure areas and using footwork.

Position

Most students, when they start to learn how to spar, want to keep their head far away from their opponent's punches. As a result, they put their head where the punch achieves its optimal velocity. Ouch! Obviously, being out of distance is a great defence. However, you can't be at a range where you can hit him, and at the same time be out of distance where he can't hit you. Therefore you've got to understand the science of slipping and body evasion.

At the furthest range of his punch your opponent only has to move a couple of centimetres at the shoulder to cover a huge range of any evasion that you could manage. Like a guided missile, he can track you, and if one punch doesn't get you, the next will.

Come closer, and the balance of power is equalized. He has to move more at the shoulder (or lower down in his body) to track you. Once you are at, or past, his elbow, he has to do lots of work to focus his tools on you. Conversely, you only have to do a little. Your positions are now reversed – you are the hunter.

You also need to take velocity into account. At long range, his arm has been accelerating to achieve maximum velocity when it hits you. The closer you get, the less time the punch has had to get going. It can still hurt, but the tighter position and angles at closer range mean that often you are slightly off the optimal angle. Think of this as 'eating his punch'. Sometimes, you can even deny him the punch he was going to throw by putting your head on his punching hand. Exactly what he wanted, but not the way he planned!

Body twist is very important in evasion. A simple, small twist can take your head right off of line, but still keeps your back straight and strong. Whenever you are evading, think of going forwards, rather than throwing your head off centre. Shifting your head takes you off balance, makes you easier to hit and makes you more likely to get knocked down by even a passing blow. Keep a strong structure at all times; back straight, focus forwards, and with the idea of putting your head as close as possible to his armpit. Go back to the bob and weave drills that we did before and see how little you can do in terms of movement – just letting him miss by a tiny amount. Never evade passively: even when you're defending, see it as the start of your attack.

5.1 > EVASION, a) slip inside the jab, b) slip outside the jab.

a)

b)

5.2 > ZERO POWER AREAS OF A STRIKE, a) block a strike early in its trajectory, b) evade the path of the blow and jam it at the end of its trajectory.

a)

b)

FOOTWORK

Now let's look at ways of developing your footwork skills. Your opponent moves fastest in a straight line. It's slower for him to follow a curve. You can frustrate his 'getting set', before he attacks, in a few ways: a) by stop-hitting him, b) by using footwork to retreat out of range, or c) by curving left or right, whichever is appropriate. He may still attack, but his power and ability to penetrate will be reduced because you have come a little off line from the position you held when the attack was launched. Watch good boxers – in particular Cubans – and you'll see them moving just slightly left or right before the attack comes. It doesn't look much, but it neutralises a lot of your opponent's advantages. That's what you want, to win without seemingly working hard for it. Making it look easy is the ultimate skill.

There are four basic directions of movement possible. If you always retreat when your opponent attacks, he will factor this in and attack longer and deeper. Do this a couple of times and then, when he's going to attack, move forward. He has no attack! What you'll find is that he's in the launch phase of his attack. There's no sharp end; no warhead, so to speak. Stop-hit him, then go back to doing what you did before.

Maintaining a mix of long and short distance will mean your opponent attacks with less venom, not knowing if he'll be countered. Sometimes in this dance you have to simply move away. Don't engage. Then, when you choose, engage strongly. I re-emphasise: when you choose. Mix this 'attack by drawing' with 'stop-hitting', plus curving left and right, and you've got a basic plan. To develop from this basic plan, it pays to watch good fighters and see how they use positional control to their advantage.

ZERO POWER

Figures 5.2 a) and b) shows the zero power areas on a strike. For clarity we've used a weapon as it is easier to see, but it can be used for any body weapon. At the start of the blow you can see that there is no power. The blow increases to reach 100% of its power somewhere about the middle of the arc (though a body twist can make this go further) then it declines rapidly to zero again. Obviously the points at which you should block or jam are the points at which the attack is at zero power. You can move closer to the origin and choke or jam the blow, or use your footwork to move away from the power.

The area in front of the weapon is called the closing line as it gets smaller; the area behind is the opening line. Sometimes you can evade by using distance, and come in behind the blow into the opening line, with the resultant time advantages (see Figure 5.2b). Once there, you can choke up his next attack by jamming that arm from coming back. He will find it hard to twist his body.

IMPORTANT

Never follow the same arc being described by his body weapon as you'll get hit. Move forwards towards the centre and then rotate, if needed.

EFFICIENCY

Sparring is taxing and it pays to be efficient in your use of energy. "Do the least, with the most effect" should be your mantra here. It's just as if you were fighting in a ring, control the centre and make your opponent move around you. It gives him two opponents to fight: you, and his rapidly increasing oxygen debt. If you want to put pressure on him, you can cut him off by moving laterally and truncating his circle. When he tries to go the other way, do the same in the other direction, gradually hunting him down to restrict his area. This puts pressure on his sense of control; he'll feel hunted and consequently he'll breathe harder and use more energy. If you are in a ring, think of trapping him in the corner. Do this when you're holding the pads for training partners, too. Make them use their footwork. Conversely, realise early when this is happening to you, and either fight for domination of the centre or keep yourself out of trouble by using light, relaxed footwork with the occasional attack. If you don't, you are the nail and he's the hammer. Remind him that you are a hammer – a hard-to-catch hammer with good footwork.

CENTRE LINE

As we're talking about position, let's look at the concept of the centre line. In defence, your opponent either has to defend his centre line and leave the edges vulnerable or leave the centre line open and protect the edges. All you need to do is attack one and then the other. Fake an attack at one target and then put all your force into an attack on the other.

Sometimes your opponent expects an attack at the centre to be followed by an attack at the edge, for instance a jab and lead hook. However, if you double up your jab or do a jab and straight right you will confound his expectations. Another route would be to alternate these direct attacks with the jab and hook, or any other mix of direct and curved strikes. It's much harder for him to defend against an unpredictable mixture of strikes.

Use time delay, once you are at this stage, so that your opponent has to choose which area to defend, leaving you free to hit the one he hasn't chosen. With all these methods it's about building patterns in your opponent's head, then confounding him once they're established by breaking the pattern. Become the puppet master.

If he's attacking you, then you can keep him on the end of an extended jab, thus controlling the centre. Use footwork to maintain control, pivot to deny him entry, and pivot as he tries to curve left or right to find a way in. Use the basic retreating footwork patterns (remembering to curve) that we covered in **Fighting**. It's essential that you keep control of and are aware of the centre line.

Sometimes you can move off his centre line but still have your own focused on him. I've shown a few alternatives, following.

Even though I've been doing martial arts and sparring for forty years, I'm frequently surprised to discover new ways of attacking the centre line, be they empty hands or with weapons. So keep an open mind and realise that, no matter what you know, there's always more to learn.

5.3 > MOVE OFF CENTRE LINE, follow-up attack across their centre line.

5.4 > ATTACKING, move off line but leave your hand on the centre line. When they turn their head to track your body movement, the attack hits their open centre.

5.5 > a) BOB AND WEAVE OUT TO SIDE, follow-up with b) KICK TO CENTRE.

a)   b)

5.6 > a) SIDE STEP AND JAB, it's hard to get hit, and then b) CROSS where their defence is weak.

a)

*'Attack where they are empty,
avoid where they are full'*
SUN TSU 'THE ART OF WAR'

b)

DON'T BE THERE

I've named this the 'Scud' approach, after the mobile missile launcher which moves as soon as the attack is launched. Even quite primitive fighters will swing away at the place where the attack on them was launched. On a basic level, you need to work on using your body to launch punches, not just your arms. If the punch only comes from the arms, you leave your head in the same place and you get hit. Use your body, with the resultant head movement, to hit harder and to be more evasive without trying. The rhythm drills I showed in **Fighting** are a great way to achieve this. Your feet aren't moving, but your head moves with each punch that you do, making you a much more slippery target.

With kicks, the use of triangle footwork or the curving footwork that we covered in 'kick for kick' mean that you are rarely standing directly in front of your attacker when attacking – and if you are, it's not for long. I've listed a number of ways to launch an attack, and then be gone. Some destroy their ability to counter by sending them off-balance.

> Angled jab and rear round kick
> Thai/wide hook and rear round kick
> Jab with triangle step and cross
> Sidestep and cross
> Step across front and back kick
> Step in and lead uppercut
> Bob and weave and overhand
> Bob and weave and roundkick
> Body hook to low roundkick

These are just some of the more simple ways of using this concept, but once you've got the idea you can add it to all your training. The idea is simple yet profound: don't be there! To do some of these takes a bit of drilling to get the move smooth. Once you've got it down then you already know what to do. **Use it straight away.**

Focus on one technique at a time and make it one part of your game. Own it by doing it in all your sparring sessions. Make it your signature technique. Once everyone knows you do that, add another to confound them. When they focus on your new thing, switch back to the first thing you became famous for. Moving promptly back out of distance after your attack will also suffice in many cases. Even this basic technique needs work, as you need to retreat promptly so use drills like the single leg bounce shown here and the footwork drill below. They will get you in and out of distance quickly.

*'Self-protection
then self-perfection'*

5.7 > SINGLE LEG BOUNCE

5.8 > a-b) JAB NEAREST PAD then c) JAB FURTHEST PAD. d) move back out then JAB THE NEAREST PAD again.

a)

b)

c)

d)

USING YOUR SENSES

To be a great fighter you've got to use your senses. Don't just use your eyes. How does his footwork sound? Fractured? Skipping around, unsure, heavy? What about his breathing? Laboured, or steady? What are his rhythms? Does he wind up before an attack? Listen. Smell, Feel his body when you are in contact. Is it tense, or strong but fluid? Is he wasting energy?

How do you practise this when away from the dojo? Traditional practise would focus on development of the whole individual as part of being a civilised person. The practises of art, music, healing and so on are all are great endeavours on their own, making you a more rounded human being. In addition, they help your martial arts ability and that, in turn, helps the rest of your life. As I've said before, 'self-protection then self-perfection' is what martial arts is all about.

CHAPTER 6 Defense

Many students of fighting in the early days concentrate on attack and going forwards whereas the great fighter wants to have a complete set of skills. This involves learning the skills of footwork, body evasion and parrying and putting them together 'in the mix'. Whilst you don't want to be scared of getting hit, avoiding it is much better, and even better if you're avoiding his strikes whilst landing your own. To paraphrase the scene in the film ' The Magnificent Seven' you don't want to be 'the man with the scar but the man who gave him that scar'. Good defence is the mark of the master and worth working on diligently.

Parry and evasion sparring

*'Skilled warriors of old made themselves invincible
and then awaited their opponents vincibility'*
SUN TSU 'THE ART OF WAR'

In this chapter we'll focus on refining your defence. The way to practise defence is to suspend some or all of your attacking capability and focus entirely on defensive skills, one at a time. You could spar for three minutes using only parrying and footwork to keep you out of trouble. Just think how potent you'll be once you start adding your attacks back in. I remember seeing the lead coach for the Japanese Karate team walking towards his team members, blocking everything they threw at him with different types of hand technique, using the palm heel, the wrist and the back of the hand to divert their blows. The team were all high-level fighters, but he made them look decidedly average, and his defence techniques were accentuated by his continual movement forwards as he did it. If he could achieve this, then why not you? Let's do some preparation. First, we're going to pressure-test your rear hand defences.

REAR HAND PARRIES

Jab sparring

Put one hand behind your back or down by your side, and use the rear hand only to parry your opponent's jab. Keep the lead shoulder raised and stay in a side-on position. For this drill he'll just pulse jabs towards you, gradually increasing their frequency. Start slow and perfect the skill standing on the spot. Next, try to move forwards and backwards. Move your head a little so that you don't use the hand too much – if you do, you'll be susceptible to multiple jabs. Important: keep your rear heel raised and use the backwards bounce with the rear foot that we covered in the snap-back section to give you extra room when you require it. The rear heel should always be raised. Do this for two or three minute rounds.

6.1 > REAR HAND PARRY DRILL, a) scoop, b) parry, c) catch.

a)   b)   c)

Wall pressure drill

Stand with one foot up against a wall, edge on and with your lead shoulder raised. Use slipping and parries with the rear hand only, to defend against head blows coming from either of your opponent's hands. In addition to parries and scoops, use elbow crushes, salute defences, and the shoulder roll extensively (mentioned in **Fighting**). Sometimes, use a long guard or trapping hand to stymie their blow or put them off balance before they get started. Do two or three minute rounds.

6.2 > WALL PRESSURE DRILL, a) rear scoop, b) block or trap, c) shoulder roll, d) cross block / trap.

a)

b)

c)

d)

LEAD HAND PARRIES

Your lead hand position will initially define whether a strike is an 'outside' or 'inside' blow. Later you won't need the hand there as you'll have developed an imaginary point in space where your early warning system starts working. Remember that whatever the fixed point, your relationship to that point can also help define whether something is inside or outside.

The next thing is to understand which parries are available to you. Once you know them, or something similar from your particular style or system, then you should use them in sparring. Initially, I like to drill these as many ways as possible, against the jab and cross or in cross loop drills like we did earlier. If you can't do them slowly and on the spot,

you'll find them hard to achieve when sparring. In truth, once you use it in your sparring, no skill looks as crisp and tidy as it did on the spot! Don't worry about this, as long as you know the basics and they work then that's OK. Just make sure your mantra remains 'drill-spar-refine, drill-spar-refine', *ad infinitum*.

Find out which parries work for you at the present time, but put aside time to work the others in drills so that you develop some body knowledge of them, plan your learning of these techniques over the course of a year.

6.3 > a) OUTSIDE PARRY to b) INSERTION, close them down.

a)   b)

6.4 > a) OUTSIDE PARRY to b) SCOOP, close them down then open them up.

a)   b)

6.5 > a-b) JERK OR SCOOP, get them to overextend.

a)   b)

6.6 > a) INSIDE BLOCK (OR SHIELD) to b) ROLL, keep them out, c) then let them through.

a)   b)   c)

6.7 > INSIDE BLOCK OR SHIELD, keep them out.   6.8 > CRUSH, use elbow and fold in to spike them early.

6.9 > CRUSH, a) use elbow to crush a blow, b) then HAMMER FIST and c) CROSS.

a)   b)   c)

6.10 > a) TRAP and b) PUNCH.

a)   b)

6.11 > TRAP AT INCEPTION, before the punch is thrown.

6.12 > TRAP AFTER, as the punch returns.

ATTACKING HIS BALANCE

You can use parries to upset and influence someone's balance. This, of course, makes it more difficult for him to hit you hard. The best plan is a simple one, affect his balance in as many ways as possible. A mix of pressing and pushing, along with pulling and simple light parries which don't give them any energy to work with, works really well. If you come from a traditional or bare-handed style that uses various hand positions in kata or forms, use them – the

rotational wrist flexion used by these moves increases their effectiveness. This approach is a bit limited with gloves but you can do some of it with bag gloves on. As an alternative, think of your hands as defining the centre line and just move your head and body around this fixed point as much as possible. This leaves you vulnerable to trapping but should be used at some time as it really refines your use of energy and stops you using big arm movements in defence.

6.13 > ATTACKING THEIR BALANCE

a)

b)

c)

d)

e)

f)

g)

Start sparring slowly using these parries, blocks and traps. Add them in one at a time until you've developed your capability. Your opponent should limit some of the power in his attacks as this is skill training. However, he should keep you honest by striking at the target, and not trying to help you with false praise. A good training partner will test your defence and be rigorous but also be aware of your weak areas. To help you develop, he should go slower and come back to that weaker area repeatedly.

EVASION SPARRING

In the same way that we've practised sparring defence using parries and blocks, let's use a similar approach with evasion. Evasion is, I think, a higher skill than parrying, though both have a place in your armoury. Parries can steal time from your opponent by re-directing him or holding him in a position, and they are a good way of attaching so that you can wrench, lock or throw. However, evasion leaves all your tools available for striking and thus in many ways is a purer skill. Psychologically, evasion is more powerful than blocking as it makes the opponent feel inept and foolish. He wastes energy and time chasing air. We're going to use a couple of supporting drills which embody all of the skills that you've already practised on the spot or in motion, but test them in a more fluid way to closely resemble sparring.

Chair sparring

In this simple drill you sit on a chair, slightly edge-on. Your opponent can stand or squat in front of you and attack with any punches he likes. Keep the pace slow. It's important for you to succeed and also to see opening and closing lines and to understand the shapes that are being presented. Rock backwards and forwards so that you move in and out of distance. When he stretches to get you, go forwards within the arc of his arms. Use body twist and your head to restrict the movement of his arms or to kill his blow at its inception. This is a great drill as it forces you to focus on using just your upper body movement.

6.14 > POSTION FOR CHAIR SPARRING, note the side-on presentation.

6.15 > CHAIR SPARRING SEQUENCE, a) parry, b) slip, c) shoulder roll, d) cover & check, e) bob & weave, f) snap back.

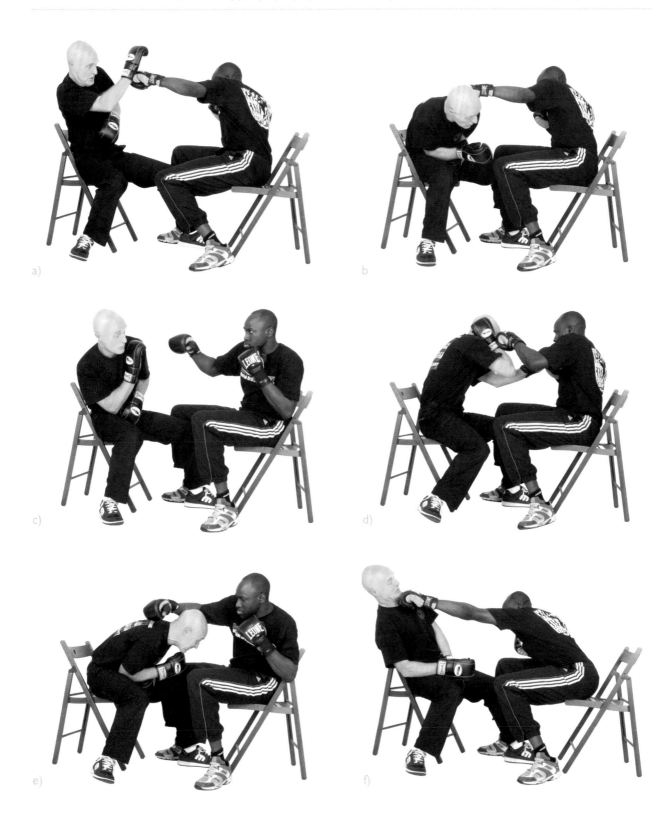

Entering

ENTERING DRILL

Start with the head-hitting drill we covered earlier. Once you are OK on the spot then try moving forwards, to put your head on your opponent's chest. Slip, bob and weave or whatever you need to do to get there. Once you have accepted the idea of occasionally getting hit, then you can adjust your slip to be much tighter. As a result, your opponent will find you harder to hit. Remember to fake one way and then go the other. Your opponent can move forwards or backwards.

6.16 > ENTERING DRILL ONE SEQUENCE, a-b) head-hitting drill, c-d) bob & weave to entry.

a)

b)

c)

d)

ENTERING DRILL TWO

The attacker walks towards you pulsing out his jab, with a loose hand only. You slip, use head evasion and as many types of footwork as you can come up with, to get to his back. Don't get fixed in thinking there's a right way and wrong way to do this. The right way is if you don't get hit and the wrong way is if you do. Of course, in hard sparring you'll be more conservative, but it's important to think, and act, out of the box. Otherwise, you are a clone and he knows already how to fight you. Be unorthodox. If you want to make it physically harder, don't attach at the waist with your arms as you take his back.

ENTERING DRILL THREE

This is basically the same as drill 2 but this time the attacker keeps his lead hand extended and in your face. As you attempt to enter, he moves backwards using good footwork so that he also gets some training benefit. This is a hard drill to do and it's hard to achieve control of the back but it's the process that's great. Here you're slipping, bobbing and weaving, using snapback and as many types of footwork as you can imagine – all together in a flow.

6.17 > ENTERING DRILL TWO SEQUENCE

a)

b)

c)

ROPE DRILL

A good way to prepare for the previous drill is to bob and weave and slip using a rope held near head-height. Initially, keep in a single stance and move backwards and forwards, bobbing either side of the rope. Then do it and change stance, letting your body twist lead your stance change.

Then add uppercuts on either side of the rope or a mix of uppercuts and overhands and hooks. Fake your head move and use slide and step or step and slide footwork. Generally, play with the drill, moving both backwards and forwards.

This works even better with good music. I favour Cuban music so it makes me think I'm training more like a Cuban boxer and I get the rhythm in my bones – but use whatever music you like.

6.18 > ROPE DRILL SEQUENCE, a-c) show bob & weave; d-f) show uppercuts.

a)   b)   c)

d)   e)   f)

Sparring format one

Now you should have sufficient skills to work with. Do general sparring using mainly evasion or smothering your opponent. In this way you are using the forwards and backwards directions we spoke of earlier in the book. Even though you're not throwing many punches, think like

an attacker – you are the hunter. Bump him, get him to overreach, follow his hand back after he punches and put your head on him. The only hand that's going to hurt you is the one that's coming out to strike you, not the one going back. Do three-minute rounds.

6.19 > SPARRING FORMAT ONE SEQUENCE, a) loose clinch, b) head control, c) evasion, d) smothering.

a)

b)

c)

d)

Corner sparring

The next type of sparring is where your opponent tries to close you down, and makes the area that you have to work in smaller and smaller. In a ring this would be the equivalent to your opponent putting you in the corner, and keeping you there so that he can unload his attack. Sparring games, where you attempt to put each other in the corner, or close each other down, are invaluable. What's important here is first to be able to fake one way and then move the other. Once you've addressed that, then you need the ability to turn your opponent once you attach and reverse your positions. There are a number of ways of doing this,

none are very easy as you have to do them in the moment. In all of this, feel where his body wants to go and seize opportunities to turn him, whatever the method.

HOOK REVERSAL

Do a left hook which is a little short and therefore ends up in front of their head. Hook your hand behind their head on the opposite side to which you would have hit. Step through, pivot and swing your opponent into the space that you've just vacated and set them up for a rear cross.

6.20> a-b) HOOK REVERSAL, c) FEND OFF to d) REAR CROSS.

a)

b)

c)

d)

CLINCH REVERSAL

Clinch with your partner in a 50/50 tie-up. Pivot and put him in the corner. You have to go with his energy so it pays to push against him to get him to push back, then reverse him.

6.20 > a-c) CLINCH REVERSAL to d) REAR UPPERCUT.

a)

b)

c)

d)

ELBOW PICK-UP

Pick up their elbow with your left arm and then transfer
to your right hand as you rotate out of position.

6.21 > a) ELBOW PICK-UP to b) move to rear, c) body hook, d) rear body hook, e) wide hook to face, f) bosh!!

a)   b)   c)

d)   e)   f)

ARM ATTACH

Attach against a strong blow, fix the elbow and pivot out
of position whilst guiding him into your former position.

6.22 > ARM ATTACH, a) block the punch, b) pull him through, c) finishing punch.

a)

b)

c)

Bob and weave

Bob and weave against a strong opponent and skip to
the left or right. Come behind him as he ploughs forwards.

6.23 > a) BOB AND WEAVE, b) curve to the left.

a)

b)

Two against one

This is a type of sparring we use for our black belt test. It can be adapted so that there is little contact and is becomes relatively safe, but it is very demanding on your footwork with the resultant improvement in skill level. You have two opponents who are both trying to get you. The art is to only let one attack you at a time. Offset the second attacker with your position so that the first attacker is always in the way of a clear attack. Don't end up where you are either in the middle between both opponents, or in an equilateral triangle with both of them having a clear shot at you. Try to move closer to one or the other. The ideal situation is where you line them up like snooker balls.

6.24 > TWO AGAINST ONE, a) angle towards one opponent, b) line them up, c) tie one up, d) clinch one opponent, e-f) manipulate as bulwark against attack, g) break free, h) continue.

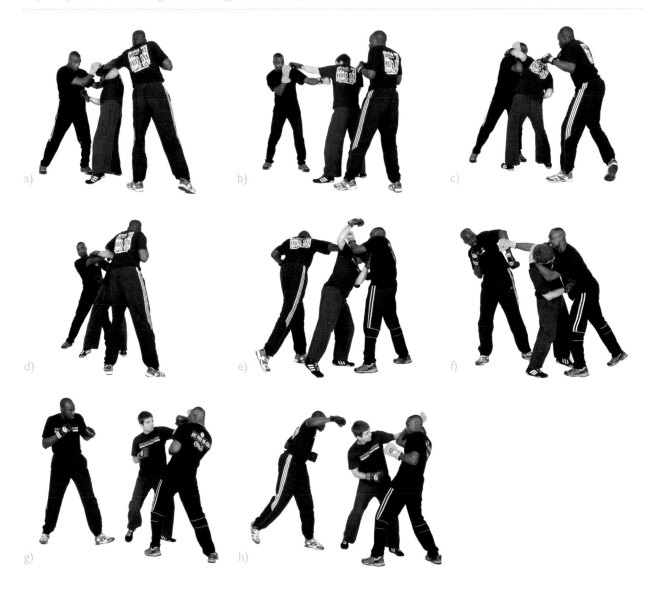

CHAPTER 7 Attack

In sparring, attack and defence intertwine. Sometimes sparring takes the form of one person attacking and one defending, but often it's a continual interweaving of the two. As a first step, it helps if you train the two in isolation. In this chapter we'll take an in-depth look at attack.

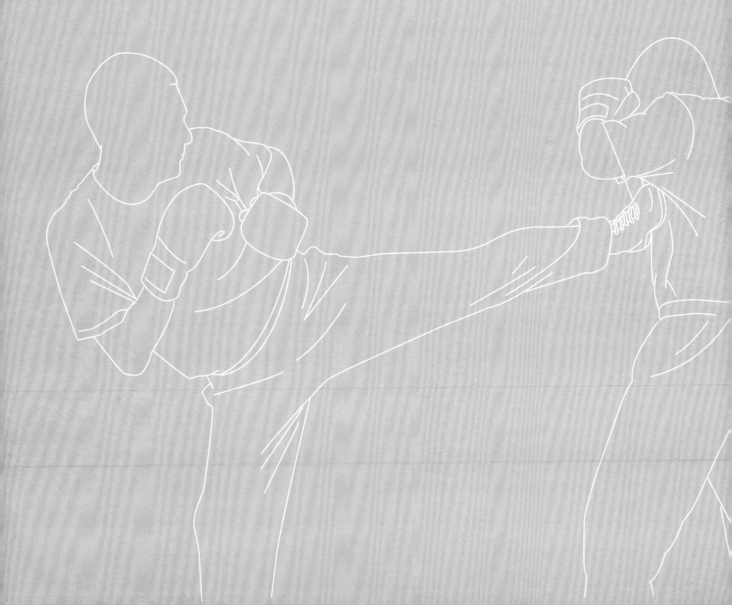

Attack

Get your mind right and your body will follow. It's good to think that you are always attacking, even when defending. Have forward intent and incline your body forward when boxing – or, at least, have your head angled forwards. Think of nodding your head, like saying 'yes' over and over again. This is amazingly positive and helps to make you the hunter not the hunted. If you are going to attack, it's important that you do it with belief and commitment. Those fighters who hedge their bets by starting to go forwards whilst also preparing to go backwards are easy to beat. The person who comes at you with a fully committed attack is scary to fight.

Obviously it's a mix. Sometimes you fake for range, or do light uncommitted strikes to see what is in his mind, but attacks from long range need commitment to work. When doing any defensive move, think of it as forming the first part of an attacking combination and you'll be harder to fight.

Bruce Lee was the highest-profile person of recent times to give a theoretical outlook on fighting in general and attacking in particular. Lee codified fighting theories that have been used by swordsmen down through the ages, but made them relevant to the modern empty hand martial artist. These aren't really concepts to think about in any conscious way whilst sparring – that sort of knowledge should be in your muscles from lots of repetition. What I recommend you do is have a one-word mnemonic like 'trap', 'crush', 'fake', that reminds you of the basic idea. The strategy you use should form itself naturally, based on techniques that you've covered in your training. What's important is to have intent, and if one method doesn't work then to have the depth of knowledge to use another way. The way to use Lee's concepts is as a way of structuring your training, so you approach each problem from a number of angles, or as a way of analysing what you have done or could do. Often you don't have to change the root physical technique that much, but seek to use it differently.

Let's look at Lee's concepts and then at ways to use them. If you find the terminology gets in your way, then re-name them. You don't even have to use them – just make sure you spar often and review your experience as you go along. They're just concepts to help you fight.

The five ways of attack are:

> **SDA** (single direct attack) or **SAA** (single angled attack)
> **ABC** (attack by combination)
> **ABT** (attack by trapping) originally called **HIA** or hand immobilization attack by Lee.
> **ABD** (attack by drawing)
> **PIA** (progressive indirect attack). This one could be called 'attack by faking'.

Let's look at them one by one.

Single direct attack (SDA)

Single direct attack is the simplest of the concept of attack, it's basically a single attacking technique done with commitment. You can angle with this and call it 'Single angular attack'. Often you follow up this type of attack with combinations, or do another SDA, or retreat out of distance and wait for your opportunity to attack again. It is vitally important that you don't telegraph your blow. Maintain a mobile base and some body movement so that it's harder for them to see your initiation of the blow.

In training, make sure that you don't telegraph blows and make sure training partners pull you up on it when you do. Pulse your hands towards your opponent all the time – it makes him less reactive as he will be less able to distinguish one movement from an actual attack. Good body position is vital if you don't want to telegraph. This almost always means getting your base right, either with your heels raised

or, if you're kicking, having the hips raised so that you have less preparation to do. This is the place to start on all techniques, whether kicking or punching. You need to be vigilant and focused on eliminating preparation from your strikes. Like a sort of infestation, no matter how diligent you are on removing problems they can creep back in, so you have to constantly keep an eye out.

Single attacks will almost always need more distance added with your feet to be successful. Achieve this either by stepping, lunging in, or hopping in after a kick. As you'll see, below, if you have to fake to cover a step then that will go under the PIA category. Remember to let your hand move first before lunging in with the feet when punching. Similarly, if it's a direct kick, when possible let the kick go first before hopping in after it. Curved or round kicks can have distance added but it's not done as often.

7.1 > SDA with a high lead round kick.

7.2 > SDA with a lead flicking jab, notice the extension on the body.

7.3 > SDA with a rear front kick.

7.4 > SDA with lead front kick.

Attack by combination (ABC)

There are going to be times when your single attack will miss so you'll need something more to back it up. In addition, a single blow often won't be sufficient to drop your opponent in a competition, or in a real fight. It's nice when it does, but don't depend on it.

ABC can mean any combination of punches and kicks. As is often the case, simple works best. Even simple combinations can be widely varied - change the timing or power structure, use alternative start points (not just the lead hand, use the rear hand or lead leg), or double up strikes on one or more of the angles. Make your method less predictable.

Orthodoxy emerges when humans study any subject. People gravitate towards a consensus, and therefore become predictable. Take as an example JKD, where many people only kick on the low line as that's seen as being most efficient (closest tool to the target). Often, as a result, they don't expect the high line kick, unless they cross train with other styles or people who do kick high. Whatever style you do, look for the orthodox or standard approach, and see the inherent strengths and weaknesses within it. Be prepared to think outside of the box. Adapt your basics, by either changing the timing or changing the power, or by coming up with novel combinations of your own. As Sun Tzu said in his Art of War, 'the orthodox and the unorthodox revolve around each other'. You need to do a mix of the expected and the unexpected. Alternatively, make the orthodox structure look different every time.

7.5 > ABC 1, a) jab to b) pendulum footwork, c) lead side kick to, d) cross.

a)

b)

c)

d)

7.6 > ABC 2, a) low line rear round kick to b) mid line lead round kick.

a)   b)

7.7 > ABC 3, a) lead leg front kick to, b) high line rear leg round kick.

a)   b)

Attack by trapping (ABT)

Many people associate attack by trapping exclusively with the famous Chinese system, Wing Chun. However, it just means that you retain or trap parts of the body so that your opponent's ability to evade, block or hit you are restricted. Trapping increases your percentage of successful hits, because a fixed or tied opponent is always easier to hit. Before I studied Jeet Kune Do or Wing Chun, I'd used hand immobilizations in Karate competitions numerous times and we had a number of what we called 'hand kills' that were a central part of our practise. It's not something unique to one style, but something that almost all systems of martial arts use in differing forms. Once you get the concept you see it everywhere. Clinch methods from both Western and Thai boxing are both examples of trapping in another form. In this book we're mainly going to be concentrating on trapping from distance as a way of entering and nullifying an opponent's defence or counter attack.

It helps to keep it simple – the KISS principle. Simple single and double traps work fabulously well and I've outlined a few here. To avoid being trapped by your opponent, keep a fluid hand structure. if you're foot trapped, realise that, in many ways, the balance of power is even. It helps, then, if you attack, though your opponent does have some advantage. If your opponent is passive, attack with a combination of blows deep inside his defensive ring or, if you desire, tackle him. A more complicated scenario happens if he hits when you trap. This is the beginning of compound trapping as practised in Wing Chun and other trapping systems. However, I've just shown a few simple ways to deal with it and to go back to your preferred theme of striking with combinations.

7.8 > ABT 1, a-b) trap opponent's jab with pak sao (slapping block), c) follow-up with back hand strike and pin / disruption, to d) rear cross.

a)

b)

c)

d)

7.9 > ABT 2. a) pak sao da and punch is blocked by defender (right). b) disengage the hand (juen sao) to double hand trap. c) jerk the arms (jut sao) and rear stomp kick. d) switched-lead cross.

7.10 > ABT 3. a) arm attachment to. b) lead pulling hand (lap sao) and cross to. c) off-balance and knee.

7.11 > ABT 4. a-b) grab lead hand and strike to. b) re-trap with withdrawing hand and strike.

a)   b)   c)

7.12 > ABT 5. a) stop on hand to, b) single trap (pak sao) to. c) body tackle.

a)   b)   c)

7.13 > ABT 6. trap with pak sao and punch and defence against cross at the same time. shown a) left side on, b) right side on.

a)   b)

Attack by drawing (ABD)

Create a tempting target that your opponent simply has to attack, or structure your body position so that your opponent has little choice but to attack you in the way you have planned. This is Attack by Drawing.

Distance is an important part of ABD, because you need your opponent to be over-committed to his attack. If you have a good footwork structure and use snap-back well, you can play a game where he is just out of distance with his attacks. In a non-verbal way you lure him in, as if to say 'if only you'd committed a bit more on that attack'. Use his greed and desire to hit you against him. When his final attack is too deep, you can simultaneously move forwards, deep inside his defensive ring, and easily counter-attack, using his momentum against him.

Psychologically, you can draw him with your idea. Often, opponents reply with the same strike that you've just used on them. For instance, where you throw a jab and

he responds in kind, you can rip a cross and body hook in because you knew in advance that he'd coming back with the jab. Essential skills here are the snap-back, against hand-strikes, and the body tuck, for straight kicks.

A common tactic I use here is called 'bait and wait', often from a position where I've got some hand contact and a good position. It's just like fishing: you have to have some patience and an understanding of your opponent. Sometimes you have to leave early from this position as he's forming some other strategy against your position. However, bait and wait works against fighters at all levels. Sometimes it has to be very subtle. If you keep the energy in your hand, your opponent won't respond and will sense the trap. You have to give a believable performance that you've missed and are depleted. His opportunistic self-belief then becomes his undoing.

7.14 > ABD, a) a high open guard to draw attacks to the exposed centre line and body, b) a high closed guard to draw attacks mainly to the body, c) a half guard drawing attacks to the apparently unguarded side of the head and body.

a)   b)   c)

Progressive indirect attack (PIA)

Progressive indirect attack was Bruce Lee's way of describing the method of entering (or breaking into a closer range), either by faking your way in, or hitting minor targets on your way to your major goal. Thus it was progressive as it moved forwards closing the range between you and your opponent, and it was indirect in that you didn't just lunge in to attack your major target like you would in SDA. I often find students get confused by the terminology of the five ways of attack – this one in particular. Change the term to suit you. See it as faking your way in, or as minor to major, and you'll take it on board more easily.

I've shown a few simple ways to make it work. Often this involves using your closest tool against the closest target. Use this principle throughout your sparring to give you half beat hits and make you a more efficient fighter.

What you'll find with the five ways of attack is that techniques can often be viewed under a number of banners simultaneously. An attack can be ABT and PIA at the same time. Don't worry about this! The aim is to get better at fighting, not to spend your time debating whether it should be defined as one or the other. Leave that to those who don't fight - you're learning to spar.

7.15 > PIA 1. a) fake low jab to, b) high head hook.

a)

b)

7.16 > PIA 2, a) jab to, b) oblique kick to, c) high line lead round kick.

a)　　　　　　　　　　b)　　　　　　　　　　c)

7.18 > PIA 3 – TRIPLE BLITZ, a) cross followed by, b) lead, c) cross to finish.

a)　　　　　　　　　　b)　　　　　　　　　　c)

7.19 > PIA 4, a) fake high to, b) low line jab to, c) high line lead hook.

a)　　　　　　　　　　b)　　　　　　　　　　c)

CHAPTER 8 Close quarter

Many students find close quarter one of the most challenging areas of sparring. In close-range sparring the tempo, timing, rhythm and fear variables make everything much harder to do. There are so many options at close quarter that any list that I devise won't come close to covering all the possibilities. Let's concentrate on close quarter boxing, although bear in mind that boxing can be countered easily by head control, tackling and throwing. However, I believe close quarter boxing gives you more than just the techniques involved, it helps your ability to deal with the pressure of fighting in general.

I've included here some of the common drills I use and some simple common patterns for striking. None of these are new and there are innumerable variables but if you haven't done this before a little help goes a long way. Most people have no knowledge of fighting at close range, so let's look at a good method to introduce the format in a formal and controllable way. We'll take one of the drills we used before – the cross loop drill – and show how to mix that in with another close quarter drill – the body hook-head hook loop drill – and use those two as a starting point.

Mixing the cross- and hook- loop drills

There are two basic loop drills that I use to get my students working at close quarter. The idea is to start with a longer range drill, the cross-loop drill (previously covered) and to combine it with a new drill, the hook-loop drill, to break into close range. Start the cross-loop drill as before by throwing a cross which he defends against and replies with his own cross and run through a few cycles before moving on. Then when you get to a position where your right hand is just about to retreat and is just underneath his attacking hand, do a short salute-type block (or cover and body hook) and then follow this with a head hook. Your partner should respond, in kind, with the same combination of blows – body hook to head hook – and this continues into a looping drill. This seems very simple but there are lots of little things happening here that make a difference to your ability at close quarter.

First is position. Imagine that you're performing the hook loop drill around a short tree stump. You have two options: you can either both go round the tree stump, moving in increments each time as you attack, or you can stand on the tree stump so that he has to move around you. Which do you think makes him work more and reduces access to your targets? The answer is obviously the one where you control the centre. In the following images, notice how my head is close; I'm checking his rear hand very slightly with my rear hand so that he can't hit me with a big cross whilst I'm hooking. You muffle his cross with your lead hand when he's body hooking you. However, if both of you make all these checks all the time, the drill falls apart. In sparring you'd feel the wrong energy and just do something else or move to a different range. Used sparingly, this drill hardwires you to check the next possible blow, without being thoughtful or conscious of your action. It's just something you do.

Second, once you're controlling the centre, look at his balance. His head is no longer on top of his base. Foot trapping or simple pushing will take him off balance, leaving him vulnerable to striking.

CROSS LOOP AND HOOK LOOP COMBINATION

You can return to the cross-loop drill by simply bobbing and weaving under his head hook, simultaneously taking yourself out to a longer range. Fire off your rear cross and you're back into the cross-loop series we covered earlier.

You need to practise this, but each time you do it you'll notice other techniques that you can use. The hardest part about close-quarter sparring is getting to or finding the reference points that you need to initiate techniques. This is why slow sparring is so beneficial, you are under less pressure, and you start to see the common shapes that present themselves.

8.1 > CROSS-LOOP DRILL, a-f) demonstrate the cross-loop drill, where the training partners try out a range of defensive moves against a cross, in a cyclic manner.

a)   b)   c)

d)   e)   f)

8.2 > HOOK-LOOP DRILL, from the cross-loop drill, await a suitable cross, then a) slip and salute / cover, to b) body hook, to c) head hook. Note, the loop continues with the partner returning a body hook, head hook, combination.

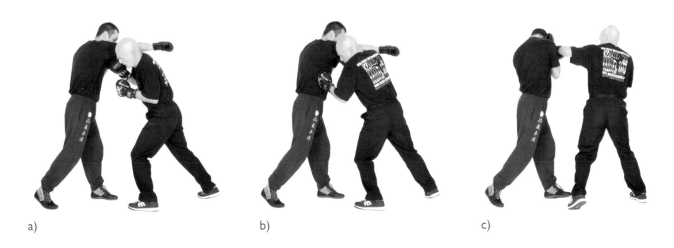

a)   b)   c)

8.3 > CROSS LOOP AND HOOK LOOP COMBINATION, a) shoulder roll, b) outside parry, c) salute cover, d) body hook, e) head hook, f) reply with body hook head hook combination, g) bob and weave under hook, h) come up fast and smooth, i) cross.

a)

b)

c)

d)

e)

f)

g)

h)

i)

Reference points

Before we start, let's look at the positions where you commonly find yourself. Bruce Lee called the points where your bodies meet or are momentarily joined 'reference points'. Not all reference points are equal. In some cases, at close quarters, you can rest, or take control of the opponent's timing or speed. You can tie him up, restrict his movement, or just be in a position that's hard to hit. There are numerous positions at close quarter and it helps to know how to strike or manipulate his balance from all of them.

8.4 > NEAR THEIR ARMPIT, a) near their right armpit, b-c) near their left armpit (often in salute or cover position).

a)   b)   c)

8.5 > OUT OF DISTANCE, a) shoulder roll and rear catch, b) snap-back and cover. Think of this a bit like being elastic, springing out of range when they punch and clinging as they return.

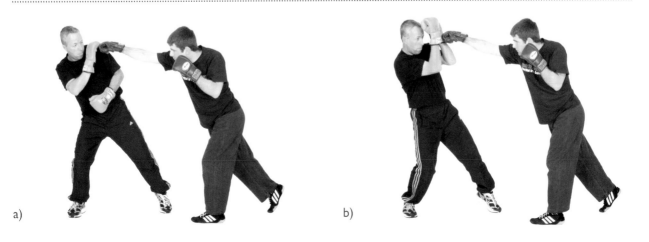

a)   b)

8.6 > SINGLE ARM WRAP, a-b) shown from two points of view.

a)

b)

8.7 > HEAD CHECK, head in the middle on their chest, or in the neck notch.

8.8 > DOUBLE BICEPS CHECK

8.9 > FIFTY-FIFTY TIE UP, equal position where both individuals control the neck and arm or their opponent.

UNDER HIS LEFT ARMPIT

The loop drills we covered earlier put you under, or near, your opponent's right armpit. Now let's look at techniques that work under or near his left armpit or shoulder. I'll assume a half-guard position here (the standard guard, to an extent, can get in your way). Remember, though, that this book is only a guide. If you find the standard guard works for you, then that's great. From the half-guard you have a number of options that come up all the time. Make sure that your stance and footwork capability is still there and that you can move with your opponent.

If you are going to break the connection between you, this needs to be your choice, and controlled by you. If he controls it and chooses the time, he's going to be punching you hard as he breaks away or bumps you to a longer range.

Think of close quarter fighting like this: if you can see his hand, his hand can 'see', or hit, you. Hide your head and, metaphorically-speaking, think of putting your eyes into your fists. Then just attack or counter-attack as you see fit. You don't have to look to see what target you've hit. The 'eyes', or sensitivity, in your hand will tell you well enough whether you've hit a good target or not. The more you trust all your body to give you real feedback, the better you'll be as a fighter. Your hands are incredibly sensitive and will tell you all you need to know, the more you trust them. Hide your head and give him the problem.

A simple plan

Here are some simple things that work well at this position near his left armpit. There are many more sophisticated techniques you can apply, but this isn't a technique book – it's about giving you strategies and tactics backed up by occasional technical tips. Once you are used to the basic position then you can use various techniques from any system you know.

8.10 > ATTACH AND HOOK, a simple way to start off working near their left armpit is when you slip or bob to the right under their jab. Attach lightly at his elbow with your head/shoulder, and left-hook his body or head. When they block one, just attack the other target. If they can cover these blows, they have to be open to other blows like the rear uppercut. Failing that, employ a strategically-timed jerk of their lead hand to open the way, and then dispatch them with a good cross or overhead.

a)

b)

8.11 > KIDNEY SLAP, they're trying to hide their head, as are you. Use a simple pivot and kidney slap to raise their head and provide you with the ability to get in a good head shot with a cross. Follow-up with shots such a body hook.

a)

b)

CREATING SPACE

If you are keeping close, you need to know how you can create space without opening yourself up to a strike. Sometimes you have to let your opponent think that you are up against the ropes or against the wall and that you can't move backwards any further. You've got three options here to create space – first, using your feet (specifically the rear foot), second, move him (bump) and third, using the space within your body shape.

Snapback

Let's look at the first option, where you use your foot position or stance to create the space. Push your rear foot back so that you've still got some room to manoeuvre, even though it doesn't feel like it to him. When you feel his forwards pressure, initially respond to it by pushing back. When you feel it, you snap or drop back and slide an uppercut or hook in the space you've created.

Bump

Use a rear foot push, with a dynamic shoulder barge, to create space and deliver your uppercut or lead hook.

Twist / internal space

It can be very effective to use body twisting to create space out of nothing, just by changing your body shape. Lean into your opponent, then twist your body quickly, retreating the lead shoulder and bringing the rear hip forwards to shoot an uppercut in the space you've created.

8.12 > CREATING SPACE, a) bump them or drop back, to b) rear uppercut; c) using body twist to create space.

a)

b)

c)

FIX THE BODY

This is really simple to do, and a great way to fix his body so that the head is easy to hook. Drop your weight and position yourself in a sort of duck, then give a quick flurry of short

blows to the abdomen. Keep the palms downwards and do four or six short shots and immediately then left hook to the head. The head is almost always easy to hit.

8.13> FIXING THE HEAD, a) high line jab, b) drop low, c) rear cross, d) lead body hook, e) rear cross, f) lead high line hook.

a)

b)

d)

c)

e)

f)

HEAD IN THE MIDDLE

When your head is in the middle (centre line), you're often coming in low under blows and need to have a simple strategy that works. You are always vulnerable to knee attacks – that's one counter to this position that you have to be aware of and have in your own defensive armoury. If you are in this position, you either have to strike or default to double biceps check or some other sort of clinch. Let's look at striking first.

First I show it in attack and then show how to defend against that position.

Heads up

Countering a person who puts their head in the middle of your chest can be done in two ways. First, do a flurry of small uppercuts with the palms up, against an opponent who's trying to enter or keep close and hide his head. Do four or six upwards from low to high. The flurry progressively brings his head up until it's in the right spot for you to left hook.

8.14 > HEAD IN THE MIDDLE, a) fake to enter, b-c) flurry of blows to the stomach, c) hook to head. Also see page 39.

a)

b)

c)

d)

UNDER HIS RIGHT ARMPIT

This is a common position and the same one as we used in the cross-loopintohook-loop drills, that were introduced earlier. There are numerous ways to get to this position. You can slip a punch, bob and weave under, snapback and follow it back, double hand control and so on. Let's look at striking options.

Body hook, head hook

As we did before, hook to the liver and repeat to the head. Alternatively, double up on the body shots and lay your head on his upper arm or shoulder to pin him in position. This buys you time.

8.15 > UPPERCUT TO OVERHAND OR CROSS, a) throw a short uppercut to his chin at an angle from which he can't see it coming, b) follow with an overhand blow or cross to the face and, if necessary, finish with a hook to the head.

a)   b)

8.16 > STEP ACROSS THE BASE, a) do the same sort of attack as in 8.14, b) step across his stance to unbalance him and open him up, c)take whatever targets are offered. Mix hands and legs if possible.

a)   b)   c)

DOUBLE HAND CONTROL OR BICEPS CHECK

Double hand control provides you with numerous techniques for controlling and striking an opponent. It's interesting that most of the wooden dummy techniques from Wing Chun end with this position, indicating its relevance. In the simplest of scenarios, you need to check his hands at the outset before he gets going, or when you see the position come up. Gain outside control of the hands to either move his body left or right. Pull and then push him, scoop for the inside line and strike, or pull down to body tackle as he lifts up. Sometimes, when you move to the inside line or are forced there, you end up in double biceps control. Let's look at simple striking from all these positions. Often when playing double hand control it deteriorates into double biceps as part of a general clinch structure.

8.17 > DOUBLE HAND CONTROL

8.19 > DOUBLE HAND CONTROL TO KICK

a)

b)

c)

8.20 > SWINGING DOUBLE HAND CONTROL TO BODY TACKLE, a) control both hands, b) swing him one way as a fake and then go the other, c-d) to body tackle.

a)

b)

c)

d)

8.21 > PULL AND THEN PUSH, a) jerk his hands towards you whilst, b) sharply dropping your body weight with the legs (don't use your arms to power this as you can be countered), c) as soon as he reacts, push his arms from underneath to open his lower lines or, d) drop back and low kick at the start of your combination attack (alternatively you can retain his hand so that he can't go too far and be out of your range).

a)

b)

c)

d)

8.22 > DOUBLE BICEPS CONTROL, a) from double biceps you can go into head control and knee, or wrap one of his arms whilst checking the other. Grab and knee, and b) simple uppercut patterns work well from here.

a)

b)

Kicking at close quarter

You can kick and knee at close quarter. Your opponent will often be surprised if you kick him well from within this range. As I've said earlier, long knees will keep a good boxer at bay, so it pays to have this down as a skill. Try to make kicking at close range a strong part of your game. As the pad holder comes towards you, closing you down, practicing by kicking against pads. Also, kick with round kicks when you are attached on the top level. Curve your body and let the kick drop onto his leg. If you've got good flexibility, you can bob and weave to the left and then kick him in the head or body with your right kick.

8.23 > a-c) KICKS AND KNEE FROM MID-RANGE

a)

b)

c)

8.24 > KNEES AND KICKS FROM HEAD CONTROL, a) knee to thigh, b) shin kick to thigh, c) stomp to thigh, d) stomp to instep.

a)

b)

c)

d)

Taking the back

Though common in MMA I've used 'taking the back' mainly as a way of letting you know that your corner has been turned and your flank exposed. The aim at all times is to retract your tools quickly and keep your striking triangle pointed directly at them.

The back is a great place to attack. Attack it after attaching in a body tackle position or simple slip position and then move to the back so you can throw, choke or continue your attack in some other way. Often if you block or scoop his

kicks, your route to the back is easy as he's in a semi-turned position. When moving to the back, you need to remember to watch out for spinning techniques. Keep your guard high and head close to his spine – not up, where it can be hit. I remember that most of the techniques that really got me when I was competing were spinning techniques. Because I was a counterpuncher I often walked into a spinning elbow, a backfist or a spinning back kick. They all hurt and are really good ways of dropping your opponent. So make sure you use them against him and don't get caught yourself.

8.25 > SCOOP TO REAR CONTROL AND KNEE BUMP, a) scoop his round kick, b) pass the leg through to turn your opponent, c-d) take his back, e) bump and lift opponent to, f) takedown to floor and grappling range.

a)   b)   c)   d)   e)   f)

8.26 > ARM DRAG FROM DOUBLE BICEPS CONTROL TO REAR DRAG DOWN, a) establish double biceps control, b) underhook his lead arm, c) drag his lead arm through to d) take his back, e-f) hip lever takedown to the ground.

8.27 > SLIP TO FAR SHOULDER PULL, a) slip his jab, b) simultaneously strike to his solar plexus, c) move to his back and c) turn him using far shoulder, to d) follow-up combination strikes.

a)

b)

c)

d)

CHAPTER 9 Body

There's the old saying in boxing: 'Kill the body and the head will die'. Body punches can be an invaluable part of your sparring toolkit. Normally, they don't carry as much power as kicks, but if you get this area down then close-quarter work is much easier. Think of body-only sparring as the nursery slopes of close-quarter boxing. All the same principles apply: it's just that you're not getting hit in the head as an additional pressure.

Targets

What targets to hit when attacking the body? The body isn't symmetrical and it doesn't pay to hit both sides equally. There are three main targets when body punching.

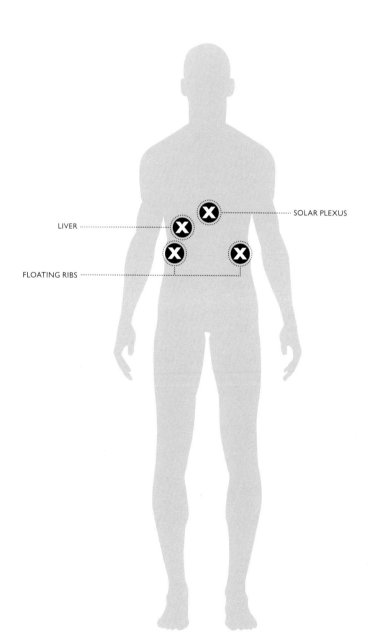

LIVER

SOLAR PLEXUS

FLOATING RIBS

RIBS

The ribs, especially the floating ribs at the very bottom of the rib cage, are good if you attack with bare hands. With gloves on, though it still hurts and may knock the wind out of your opponent, you've got to have good punching power and skill to drop them in one hit.

SOLAR PLEXUS

This is a great target to hit but you need to practise hard to make sure that you are consistently on target, or very close. You can hit this with straight punches and shovel hooks, they are both very effective. Most people aim too high and hit the chest.

THE LIVER

The liver is the biggest organ in the body and is a great target to hit. Other organs, like the spleen and kidneys, are deeper in the body and generally can take a lot more punishment. I've tried targeting the kidneys and back, both in sparring and on the street, and though it can stun an untrained person, it's not a high percentage area. Why waste your time on lesser targets – unless it's to set your main target up?

Many people haven't ever been hit in the body, so hitting it anywhere is a good way to set up follow-up strikes to the head. When you hit the body, people tense up and become less fluid and mobile. It's almost like they wait for the body to provide a damage control report before moving, the result being that you can hit his body and then switch to attacking the head.

Before we move on to attacking in general, let's work on defences for body punches. There are a number of simple methods that work well. However no method works well for long, so you have to ring the changes or knock them out as soon as possible, otherwise you'll be in trouble.

Techniques

Start these as two-man drills, with one person attacking and the other defending. The techniques can then be looped together so you've got body-only sparring, with one person attacking and the other defending. Even though you're not hitting back, it's still sparring. Start like a drill and then as soon as you've got it down you can freeform it.

ELBOWS

Against straight blows, use a standard guard and use your elbows to block. Move them forwards at a slight angle, to jam or block the opponent's blows. Don't move them across your body, which will open up other lines of attack. Remember your eyes, keep them focused on the opponent and not on the blows coming at you. The attacker initially attacks with left and right hand straight blows to the centre of your body. Later, he can double-up or do them in any order he likes.

9.1 > ELBOW DEFENCES AGAINST STRAIGHT BLOWS, remember to move your elbows forward to cut into their blow, not across your body.

a)

b)

CROSS GUARD

The cross guard is an excellent defence. Think of it as having two of everything: two elbows to spike his blows, two hook punches just ready to go, two hands to grab, hook his hands and immobilize them or pick up his elbow and manipulate him out of position. When you've practised, it gives you crushing, trapping and attacking skills. This guard also works against uppercuts. It forms a bar, which means he can't uppercut without being blocked – he's got to look for another way if he wants to attack your head up the centre line. The weakness of this position is that its horizontal shape makes it susceptible to trapping if used at the wrong distance.

9.2 > CROSS GUARD AGAINST STRAIGHT BLOWS, a) against a jab, b) against a cross, c) hook his hand to open him up for strikes, d) cross to follow-up.

a)

b)

c)

d)

HALF GUARD

Deny him a good direct target. Move the guard around so that whatever attack he does, he strikes your arms. You can sometimes adapt this, if doing it with bare hands, and let him strike your elbows. It spikes his hand and takes some of the vigour out of his blows. Even though we're not hitting the head here, keep your lead shoulder up and be prepared to shoulder roll. I know we said body-only but sometimes people forget!

9.3 > HALF GUARD, a) elbow block, b) arm block, c) elbow spike, d) elbow deflection, e)-f) body twist left and right.

TWIST

Simply twist so that the body part they are attacking is the facing the other way. Train all of these skills first in a drill format but, as soon as you can, use them free form. If you get problems, go back and refine the skill through repetition. Play with it at progressively faster speeds. This will make you realise that you have to establish control to make things go at the pace you want. Look at controlling the opponent and his use of space by pushing him backwards with your presence or by turning him. Your aim is to make him seem inept.

ELBOW CHECK

This seems unlikely but works really well. Derived from Filipino blade fighting where you try to stop the opponent from drawing his weapon, it works just the same here. You wait for him to punch with the rear hand. As he goes by, just attach to his elbow and you've killed his next blows. When he goes to counter your check, just take it away, and then replace it. It's very frustrating for your opponent, and you have great control over his body.

9.4 > ELBOW CHECK, a) as his cross goes past you, attach at his elbow, b) check his elbow into his body to kill follow-up blows.

a)   b)   c)

DOUBLE CHECK

Do this when he's regrouping and just about to start. Pin both of his hands or cover his lead and pin the other to his body. If he twists to get away you can reverse the position. You can't stay here for more than a few seconds but it's about having control and negating his game. From these positions you can attack his base or arm drag or kick as the start of a combination attack.

9.5 > DOUBLE CHECK, a) double check, b) arm drag, c) step across his base.

a)   b)   c)

BAR

Use your forearm to create a central bar across his body. Think of it like an extended half-guard. This works well against those using standard guards because you can jam all of their options. Often they'll push back against you. This opens an opportunity for a sharp left hook and pin, whether you are inside or outside their guard. Repeat as necessary.

You can also grab your opponent's arm as he pushes into you, and hit him with your rear hand as the start of a combination. You can then use this extended arm that you've hit with (right hand) to bar your opponent again on the other!

9.6 > BAR ACROSS OPPONENT'S GUARD

a)

b)

9.7 > LEFT HOOK TO BAR

a)

b)

9.8 > BAR TO RIGHT CROSS

a)

b)

Routes to the liver

The liver is one of your main targets to attack. If you watch lots of boxing matches you'll often see the loser get hit with a good liver shot and then, within a couple of moments, go down from a right cross or other blow. Think of it like a sinking boat getting torpedoed again to finish the job. A friend and I would spar regularly on a Saturday morning and finish with body-sparring, focused on liver shots. The agreement was that whoever got dropped by a liver shot had to buy lunch. This was a great motivator, and surprisingly funny to do even if you get caught. He still owes me for a couple of lunches!

SLIP LEFT AND BODY HOOK

This is the simplest method to access the liver. You slip to the left, and hook or shovel hook to the liver. Remember you can go around with the hook and let it hit the back of the liver, or use the shovel hook on the frontal lobes where it pokes out from below the ribs. Sometimes your opponent comes to you by doing a big cross that misses and you just take the opportunity offered as the line opens up. Other times you'll have to work for it. Warning: sometimes when you slip like this you are also in a great position for them to do the same thing to you. So don't be too greedy or predictable. If you lean out over your lead leg you can often hit the liver nearer the back. It enables you to hit both the front and rear targets, so making it more difficult to counter or block.

BOB AND WEAVE

Think of your position near the liver as a favourite restaurant you like going to. You need a number of routes to get there depending on where you start from, but the food is always good. Here you just bob and weave under his cross and you're there with plenty of time to spare. Make sure you have good balance by having a forward focus, and don't take your head too far off line.

'Seize opportunity by the forelock'
MIYAMOTO MUSASHI

9.9 > BOB AND WEAVE to liver shot.

a)

b)

ATTACH AND MOVE HIM

Use two hands to attach to his arms. Shift both of his arms to the right to expose the liver. Try also using the left or right hands only to steer him to your right. If using the two hands approach, you can fake one way so he reacts against it and then go the other way to achieve your goal.

9.10 > ATTACH AND MANIPULATE, a) attach with both hands, b) manipulate both arms to the right to expose the liver, c) use or left hook or shovel hook to strike to the liver.

a)   b)   c)

SALUTE

Slip to the left as before, but use a salute block to keep his ribs open whilst you attack. Think of lifting and separating the ribs, whilst lifting his top away from his base.

9.11 > a) SALUTE and b) BODY HOOK.

a)   b)

OVER THE TOP

Sometimes if he's coming at you strongly and his head is
down and forwards, you can lean over him and just hook
straight to his liver. In this way you are using a route that
comes over the top. Hitting the rear quadrant of the liver is
less effective than hitting the front but it's still a great target.

9.12 > LIVER SHOT FROM OVER THE TOP.

a)

b)

SUMMARY

Now we've covered body-work in depth. When working this area of sparring, don't neglect the integration
of your head-defence skills. Keep all of your skills working as part of the whole toolkit you're building.
You don't want to have two separate games: rather, one game that has different focuses. Once you've
got one area down, put it back into the whole. Use body rotation, snapback, the four directions and
sometimes just move away to have a rest. Better still, attack him with your balance and position so that
he has to go away for the rest. Then you're ahead psychologically. You're the hammer and not the nail.

CHAPTER 10 Opponent control

Here we're going to look at ways of making your opponent obey your commands and do the things you want, or act in ways that you can easily predict. Once you know how to do this you'll be more successful and your level will improve. In the end it's like a chess game. Fighting solely as a physical skill can soon lose it's thrill but outsmarting your opponent is hugely rewarding.

Faking, feinting and deception

No matter how good your skill, a strategy that relies only on a direct approach will soon get you soundly beaten. To increase your success rate, you have to learn how to fake or feint. It's very easy in fighting to roll out some of your training practise and perform your attack 'on the beat'. Remember that your opponent may also have been training, so he knows the routine. Do you really want him to crush your hardest round kick?

It's important to add a number of variables to your combative mix. Let's first look at angles, then at pre-programming them and then at timing.

10.1 > FAKE HIGH AND ATTACK LOW, a) fake with high round kick, b) drop the kick to attack lower leg, c-d) continue to lower leg drag.

a)

b)

c)

d)

ANGLES

Your opponent can't cover all the angles all of the time. Use variations of attacks to the high or low line, the inside, centre or outside lines.

High and low

The further apart these two poles are the better. If you're faking high, make sure you do it either at or even above their eye line and then come in low for your next attack. If you're going to fake low then make sure you actually go low, drop your body – don't just drop the arm. You'll see why later! Then follow-up with your high punch or kick. If you're using kicks, make sure you touch the low-line knee area to get a response, and then proceed higher.

In and out

Similarly, you can attack the centre line as a fake and then do your real hits to the edges, or vice versa. Wide hooks to the head or body work well here. Remember you can hit up and down the centre-line with straight blasts, shovel hooks, uppercuts and overheads.

PRE-PROGRAMMING

An opponent relies on his senses to build a model of his combative world. This allows him to predict what is going to happen. You therefore need to control some of the input his senses receive, and sell him the wrong information. Think of yourself as the puppet master and him the puppet. How do you do this? Let his imagination and pattern recognition software work on your behalf.

Pavlov three

Pattern recognition tends to work in threes. It takes two repetitions for your opponent to start to recognise a pattern. I call this the Pavlov three. Repeat something strongly twice and he begins to imagine a pattern forming. You don't have to hit him, you can hit his glove as this is safer for you. However, you have to convince him that you have the capability to hit him and his brain will do the rest. Just like viewing an abstract painting, the brain will fill in the gaps. You need to allow three or four seconds to let him ponder what could happen to him: such a 'what if' scenario needs time to rove around his brain. You initiate the third blow just as you did with the previous two. For instance, perhaps you started with two stiff jabs to his heart area. If he's parried the early two, cut the third one short – this will bring his parry further out to complete the sequence or mental loop that's happened before, leaving another line open to attack (in this instance, perhaps for a left hook to the jaw). His expectation of a pattern will work to your advantage. Another good example would be, starting with a low groin or inside leg kick. You attack to get him to respond and to build his anticipation of another similar attack. Build it with two hard kicks and then on the third one start in the same fashion, but change to a head kick half-way through. Beware, sometimes he can use this against you by breaking his own defensive pattern. On the third punch he just hits you instead. So it's important to be threatening throughout.

'Avoid where they are full,
attack where they are empty.'
SUN TSU, 'THE ART OF WAR'

10.2 > RIGHT UPPERCUTS TO LEFT UPPERCUT, a) sell him on your right uppercuts, repeat twice with hard blows, then switch to b) left uppercut

a)

b)

10.3 > FAKE ROUND KICK TO FRONT KICK, a) start by throwing two round kicks, then let him see your foot go out as if to perform a third, b) when your legs gets to the blind spot near his guard, switch to a penetrating front kick.

a)

b)

CURVE PREDICTION

If you hit someone, their guard acts like a grid through which they view the world. There are various blind spots so he has to predict what's going to happen by continuing the curve of the blow you've shown you've started. He puts his defence in the place where he projects that it will land. It actually means he's faster than you – but you just make sure you sell him the wrong information. Once again, use the Pavlov three and let him know you have capability. Then start the third one and his brain does all the rest. 'Ah, I've seen this before and so I can get there early' is what goes through his brain. However, you're going somewhere else.

10.4 FAKE REAR ROUND KICK TO PENDULUM CROSS, a) fake the round kick then withdraw the leg, b) simultaneously hit with an overhand right (note, this is a big punch and easy to see unless you really sell then on the initial kick).

a)

b)

Timing

TELEGRAPHIC MOVEMENT

Your opponent will react to your body's movement. Generally the blows that kill are those supported by full body weight and motion, which tend to require larger movements. Our brains are therefore hard-wired to react to these large movements. Conversely, the brain doesn't particularly respond to small movements like those made by the limbs, otherwise you'd be reacting to everyone who waved for a taxi or who raised their hands to scratch their heads. Your body reacts to motions like a double-handed battle axe being smashed towards your head, or a steel toed boot being swung at your groin. Reactions are hardwired and no matter how much training you have, you still react to some extent. The only way to negate some of your reactions is to stop-hit or move away against all attacks.

INDEPENDENT MOTION

Ideally you need to train to use the hand and arm to do much of the movement first, and then let the body follow. Like a Ferrari, the power is in the back (foot, leg and hip) not in the front (arm and shoulder). By the time he sees the strike, it's too late. Fencers have used this principle to great effect through the ages since they developed the use of the point of the sword. Though this type of attack isn't the hardest, it makes contact more often, and hits their confidence. Mix it in with the occasional hard hit and they are chasing demons everywhere – with resultant holes in their guard.

PUT INTO PRACTICE

Jab out using only the arm, and just before making contact let the body follow, driving from the rear leg. Another example would be to use your foot jab at a longer distance than usual, just before hitting you then hop in behind the kick to add the power. For the hands think Muhammad Ali.

Now use the shoulder or hip fake to get your opponent to overreact. You know when you are doing the fake well, as he blinks or reacts to your fake. You can use the fake without a follow-up strike to make him feel a little stupid and over-reactive. He will respond by turning down his sensitivity levels, allowing you to hit him more easily. Alternatively, after using fakes for a while, so that he comes to expect them, switch to just hitting with no faking. That also makes your opponent feel a little stupid. Mix body fakes in with independent motion strikes and he won't know whether he is coming or going.

The brain has to deal with a whole range of speeds, from slow to fast, and it can't work at its best at all frequencies. It therefore concentrates on the speeds that are most crucial to its survival. It will tend to match that of the opponent being faced. Much like hunters emulate a deer to hunt deer, or people copy other people's body language to better communicate, the same happens combatively. You can get him to go slower often by going slower yourself. By matching your pulse to his, you are one person in many ways, in a sort of duet.

Once you've got them to match, then you can go in and hit him hard and fast in combination. It takes time for him to reach the new speed. When he wants to continue at speed, don't match him: just play along, with a casual game, using your footwork. Once he's calmed down, go back to your puppetry. Even easier is to be really fast and furious in your attack, you don't actually have to take too many risks as you only need to give the appearance of action (unless he's very experienced). Once you've wound him up and he's reduced his focus to just those things that are coming towards him fast, then you can walk in as slowly as you like and bash his lights out - often with only a single blow. This takes judgement but I've done this against some of the best fighters.

10.5 > PLAY WITH FAKES AND YOUR TIMING, a) hip fake, b) shoulder fake.

a)   b)

FAKING TIPS:

- **Don't hit the expected target**

- **Late is the new early**
  Just like being late for the eight o'clock train means that you're early for the nine o'clock one, realise that delay can be really advantageous. In the simple combinations that you do, add delay to radically change what's happening e.g.: jab, cross, then (delay) hook.

- **Eye eye**
  Use your eyes to sell other lines and then hit where you had originally planned.

- **Hello**
  Say hello to a non-existent person half way through your fight as if he has come into the dojo, your opponent will often turn to look. Get your cheap shot in whilst he's looking away.

- **Don't be on the beat**

- **Learn an instrument or be acutely aware of rhythm**
  Just dividing music into single, double and triple beats as you listen to it will help your understanding and feel of timing.

- **Strong fighters are everywhere, but strong, intelligent fighters aren't as common**
  Mindful awareness of the puppetry introduced in this chapter makes you a harder fighter to beat. Just be aware that not all attacks are equal and don't play into their game. If someone is playing you, just hit into all their attacks. They will soon quit their games or you will drop them.

- **When you fake it has to appear real and dangerous to your opponent**
  If it doesn't bite then you're only trying to impress, often you're trying to scare them or keep them away by doing lots of work. However, none of it means anything. On the street, 'hit' to fake, as trained responses don't work so well there.

- **Do less, but base it on hitting them (or hit them!)**
  An experienced fighter will see through 'hand waving' and attack you, knowing you are weak.

CHAPTER 11 Themes and games

I've set out a number of simple sparring games or themes. These are just a place to start and you can adapt them as you want. Do these for a while then start working out your own. You can also go from one theme to the other so that your brain is learning to adapt to changing circumstances. To make it even more interesting add different round lengths, change the length of rest periods or put circuit type action during the break and you'll challenge your cardiovascular system just like it is in the ring.

Sparring games

There are countless variations of themes and games you can play in sparring. Once you understand the concept, you can invent your own. Each of the games I introduce in this chapter has a different focus and is a good way to develop your technical skills in that area. Some of the simple ones are obvious. However, regular practise of them gives you a deeper understanding of that area specifically and of fighting in general.

We've already got two basic templates: hands only, and hands and legs. Hands-only sparring can be sub-divided into four basic types: long-range, close-range, body-only, and all-in. I've covered close-range and body-only sparring in earlier chapters as there are lots of techniques to cover and they therefore need more consideration. Hands and legs uses the same basic templates, omitting body-only. I recommend sparring mindfully. In all sparring it's important to have a focus, or an area that you are working on. I see many people who spar without any plan of where they want to get to and consequently waste their effort. Of course, sometimes it's just fun to spar. Whatever you do, it has to be fun and you have to do lots of it. Use ranges and work on your weak points in addition to your strong ones. Adapt your game to your opponent, work on differing rhythms or focus on defensive or attacking skills. Whatever you do there's lots to work on.

Start with your basic sparring and add in these technical games. Alternatively, you can start with the technical sparring games I'll outline here as an entry into free sparring. The important thing is to get started, but not to get hurt in your initial outings if you're new to the game.

GAME 1: SINGLE TOOL ISOLATION SPARRING

This game develops your abilities with a single tool. Use the sparring format that was introduced before, but this time your opponent can use any of his hand tools. You can only pick one tool to use in attack. Use just the jab initially and then try other tools.

This sounds daunting, but in fact the singular focus gives you huge advantages. What you'll find is that you are much more effective than your opponent in most cases. Good footwork and snapback are essential here. This works especially well with the jab and in my experience other tools don't work quite as well. However, you learn a lot about the tool by trying it – whether it's successful or not. Having said this, you don't want to research my experience – you want to gain your own. Maybe you'll find a 'new' way. Be humble here; lots of 'new' ways have been discovered before you came onto the planet. However, the voyage of discovery makes it more precious to you and forms it as part of your style, your personal system, and that's great.

11.1 > SINGLE TOOL ISOLATION SPARRING, a-b) the jab is used against an opponent using any technique.

a)

b)

GAME 2: LEGS-ONLY SPARRING (MEDIUM-CLOSE RANGE)

Use leg techniques only, trying to keep a constant distance from your opponent. Try not to move out of range unless it's essential; rather, move circularly. Think of it as a development from kick-for-kick. In addition to any hand parries, use the crush for all kicks up to the waist and the arms to cover yourself from there on up. Check out the crush drills in Fighting for a basic understanding of this area. Try to use multiple kicks from the same leg in addition to simple left-right combinations. Add in angling and use the extended lead hand in long guard to check his body. The 'circling the pad drill' featured in **Fighting** is a good way to move away and check or manipulate your opponent, whilst preparing to kick. Hand wrestle or manipulate his body so that you disperse some of the power of his kicks. You'll learn that, at this range, you are going to get hit. However, it's all about minimising the power with which you get hit.

Remember the zero power concept covered earlier. Add-in all your checks, pushes and pulls – and you'll get hit less often and with less power. Don't kick as hard as you can. Remember, this is a game. It's more about learning to flow and keep a continuous attack going whilst taking hits. Remember to look after your training partner: partners with broken or bruised ribs can't train with you anymore.

11.2 > LEGS-ONLY SPARRING, a) attack their posted leg, b) use a variety of angles of attack, c-d) crush all kicks to waist height.

a)

b)

c)

d)

GAME 3: LEGS-ONLY SPARRING (LONG RANGE)

Here you should attempt to use leg tools only or to mainly focus on the legs. Supporting techniques can be used to make your game more effective. Adopt a more side-on stance and you will predominantly use your leading leg, although the other leg can be used just as well. Focus on side kicks, round kicks and hook kicks, either spinning or from the back leg.

Use the hands to fake high. Use body fakes to 'sell' the wrong timing to your opponent, and then come in later or when his reactions have become worn and he's not so reactive. Back-fists work well to set up lead leg kicks and can be followed up with a lead hook.

11.3 > LEGS-ONLY SPARRING AT LONG RANGE, a) long-range snap kick, b) high round kick, c) parrying a front kick, d) axe kick.

a)

b)

c)

d)

GAME 4: HANDS AND LOW LEG SPARRING (MEDIUM RANGE)

Use all of your hand skills plus attack his legs with low kicks. Maintain a shorter stance, like a Thai boxer. Your weight distribution should be even or slightly towards the rear so that you can use your legs to crush. A simple plan is to use the lead leg only to crush both his legs, but this strategy makes you predictable. To protect the lead leg, don't extend the stance into a boxing stance like you may have used in hands-only. Rather, keep your ankles firm and the heels raised, and punch from a stiff leg. It may help if you think of it like punching over a barrel. This way your ribs are not so vulnerable to the long knee and your hips are raised so you can kick quicker and easier.

11.4 > HANDS AND LOW LEG SPARRING, a-c) use a variety of hand tools in combination with low leg kicks.

a) b) c)

GAME 5: HANDS VS. LEGS SPARRING

What you'll normally find here is that the person kicking is good at keeping the puncher away and attacking the lower legs. However, it will take longer to put kicks together into combination than the hands. Once the puncher has entered range, they can hit away and there's very little the kicker can do. Think of this as getting inside the castle: the battlements are crossed and his defences breached. This is a great type of sparring to improve range-entering skills and, for the opponent, his kicks. Make the kicks fast and don't leave them out where they can be grabbed. Integrate kicks into your whole game with good footwork. Multiple kicks work well, though you have to have good core strength. Check out the tree exercises that we covered in **Fighting** as a base from which to work. Add fake kicks to draw his defence and repeat kicks to the same target to build fear and apprehension. Don't worry if you are kicking and you don't prevail. That's not really the point, though it's great if you do.

11.5 > HANDS VS. LEGS SPARRING, a) kick used to keep puncher at bay, b) puncher enters range with a cross before the kick strikes, c) kicker re-establishes range.

a) b) c)

GAME 6: ACQUIRING HEAD CONTROL

Getting control of the head gives you a great opportunity to knee or manipulate your opponent. Sometimes called the 'plumm', this is used a lot in Thai boxing and is a core part of modern fighting due to its effectiveness. You can use whichever sparring format or game you want; your opponent can use hands-only, defence-only or all-in. Whatever he does, his aim is to gain head control and to knee. You have to keep your strikes short and sharp, and avoid his head grab with head evasion. Use your hands to keep him from attaching. Use a short and sharp foot jab to keep him at distance. If he grabs, go directly into your head control counters, don't wait for him to start kneeing. Alternatively, gain a pre-emptive head control over him and knee him.

Pressure sparring drill

As a great conditioning drill and as a way of gaining knowledge, you can use the following sparring drill. Both of you pad up. One person can kick and the other person's aim is just to grab and knee. This puts a lot of pressure on both of you. The kicker really has to work and kick, moving backwards and in rearward curves and arcs. If the kicker moves straight back, it's easier for them to grabbed and kneed. The person attempting head control has to be single-minded and unhesitant in his attacks, often after the kick has missed or even if it hasn't. Great training!

---

11. 6 > ACQUIRING HEAD CONTROL, a) parry or guide a kick across you to, b) gain head control.

a)

b)

GAME 7: ATTACH AND LIFT

Let's concentrate on attaching to throw. Think of this as either preparation for throwing or attaching for body tackles. You can do both, regardless of the hardness of the floor that you're training on, in safety. The importance of penetration and having a 'body-to-body' fit is crucial to developing your throwing skills. In this sparring, the techniques used don't matter that much. Your opponent tries to move in, grab you, and lift you from the ground. In defence you have to punch or kick, move, re-direct or use the plumm and knee to deny him the body throw. If you've got Judo experience, you can see this as sparring with Uchi Komis or entries added at the end. Get to the point at which you could throw them, and then start again.

11.7 > ESTABLISHING BODY-TO-BODY CONTACT IN PREPARATION FOR TAKEDOWNS.

a)

b)

c)

GAME 8: TACKLES

Tackles are an integral part of modern fighting and very hard to defend against, except with sprawling. Against primitive closure methods you can use blocks or re-directs but against a good fighter, tackling low, you'll find it hard to counter. Sprawl and move to the back, or 'seatbelt position' against an opponent who tackles you. Don't do this on hard floors, only on mats. The tackler does his tackle, and then assumes an all-fours position, whilst you rotate quickly to the side or rear. If possible, trap the legs with your legs to negate rolling on his part.

11.8 > MID-LEVEL, BODY AND LEG TACKLE

a)

b)

c)

11.9 > TAKING THE BACK

a)

b)

11.10 > LOW DOUBLE-LEG TACKLE

a)

b)

11.11 > LOW SINGLE-LEG TACKLE.

a)

b)

Limited sparring

We've dealt with different types of basic sparring, varying the distance that you are working at or having a themed approach to build skill. Now let's look at putting pressure on your skill base and strategic understanding, by putting limits on your sparring practise. When I had really bad hips and couldn't walk easily, the only type of sparring I could do was to stand on the spot and trade punches with whomever I was practising with. Imagine that your feet are in a laundry basket and you get an idea of the type of sparring I'm talking about. Like all these problem-based types of sparring, the more of it you do the better you get. In the end, you relish being put into a bad position because it challenges your skill to the maximum. When you put it back into the mix you're a stronger and more potent fighter.

LIMITED MOVEMENT

In this type of sparring you limit the amount of movement that you are able to do. You'll end up being a better fighter under pressure, but remember to go at the pace you can handle. Too hard and it's guaranteed to make you 'gun shy' – afraid of being hit – and that's not the aim. Let's look at a variety of options.

Fixed point

Either one or both of you have one fixed foot position which you pivot around. Much like the jab isolation sparring we did earlier, it simplifies your choices and you come to realise how much movement you can manage with the minimum of stance changes. Investigate the borders of your balance.

11.12 > FIXED POINT SPARRING, a-c) one or both partners have a fixed front foot position and use that point to pivot around, testing your movement and balance.

a)

b)

c)

11.13 > ONE FIXED POINT, Owen (right) keeps his left foot planted and moves forwards and backwards moving the right foot.

a)   b)   c)

One fixed

In this game, your opponent can move around you, but you're limited to stepping backwards and forwards with one foot, plus, employing body movement and manipulation. Of course, you can pivot, so that you keep him in your striking range. Control the centre line and make him work.

Both fixed

Take up a position near to your opponent. Each of you should place one foot on a bag glove or inside a ring of some sort, and trade punches. Remember the laundry basket analogy from earlier – we are trying to limit your foot movement. Concentrate instead on body movement and stance change to dominate or close down your opponent.

One mat

Both fighters stand on a Judo mat. The aim is to fight with medium to light power and for both fighters to stay on the mat at all costs. If you come off, you have to do some sort of punishment training like push-ups or squats, and then go back to the sparring. In the main, it's your own ego that keeps you on the mat. Often you will be dominated psychologically, not just physically. You have to resist this and stand your ground. The experience you get is invaluable.

LIMITED SHOTS

You can do this in two main ways:

First to score

Spar using a points system, akin to a Karate competition. Whoever gets to three or five targeted hits is the winner. Once there's a winner, or when the time's up, you move on to the next opponent. The loser can do push-ups or something similar as punishment. In limited shots sparring, losing should have a price. Again a third person acting as referee can be advantageous in this format.

Out of bullets

Imagine that you have a limited number of punches or kicks, just like the magazine in a gun. Once you've spent your number (five's good) then you can only defend until the time is up. Two minute rounds work fine for this. You realise you have be more circumspect and make sure you've got a good opportunity before you strike. This helps you to learn to be an efficient fighter and to keep your cool.

In all these types of sparring, keep centred. Don't be dragged into action by your opponent; the psychological pairing or copycat tendency we all have is to be fought against. Move to your own drum, not your opponent's. Keep cool, and continuously have in mind your immediate and your long-term goals.

Pressure testing

One fighter stays in the ring; the other fighters swap in one after the other, for two minute rounds apiece. Everyone benefits, but the fighter who stays in the ring gets the most from the training. You can do this whenever there are three or more of you. If there are more it's great, because not only is the main fighter fighting with a cardiovascular deficit against fresh opponents, he'll be getting different styles of fighter and have to use his brain whilst under pressure. Two minute rounds work fine here. Make the sparring light and fast. If you are going in against the person in the centre, think of keeping the pressure on him all the time. You're only there for two minutes so don't take rests, unless it's to move out of his way.

If you are the person being pressure tested, then your aim is to make the other fighters dread the end of the other person's round, as they've not fully recovered from their previous round with you. When you can keep three fighters challenged, then your sparring fitness is at a really high level. In addition to the basic sparring templates, you can use any of the skill-focused formats we've covered against the rotating opponents, or think of your own. After all, who knows what you need to focus on better than you?

11.14 > LINE UP PRESSURE TESTING, the centre man spars a line of opponents each for two minute rounds, knowing that a fresh opponent is coming on at the end of each round

CHAPTER 12 Strategies

Anyone who has been sparring for a while will have noticed that each individual, even within a dedicated system, has different natural attributes, skills and style. Each will potentially offer a unique learning experience. The intelligent fighter will seek out new experiences to test, develop and adapt their own skill set. Let's look at how to deal with some common problems that arise in sparring.

Strategies

THE TALLER OPPONENT

If you are shorter than your opponent and he has a long reach, you've got quite a significant problem. He can keep you on the end of his jab and make you pay a high price to enter. There are a number of basic strategies that you might use to overcome this challenge.

If you're the person who's taller or has a longer reach, keep your opponent at the end of your jab - he has to slip to get to you. As he goes under, give him your next range of techniques like the shovel hook or the long knee.

12.1 > BE QUICK AND ELUSIVE, attack with non-committal quick strikes to annoy him so that you draw his jab or cross. Once he gives you a committed strike, slip and attach lightly, so you are linked to him and he can't retreat to distance. Follow his strike back and hide under his armpit. Once you're in, lead-hook to his open lines.

12.2 > DRAW HIM, offer up easy targets, which are just out of reach. Draw him a couple of time so that he just falls short and has to commit a bit more with each attempt. Eventually he will over-commit and you can counter.

12.3 > CRUSH HIS ATTACK; use your elbow, moving inwards with one of your hands covering his other hand. If he kicks, it's harder for him to recover and gain distance again, so he's unlikely to do that.

12.4 > FAKE AND DROP YOUR LEVEL, a) attack with your body held high so that you attract a counter on the high line, and then b) drop your level half-way through your attack. Use slide-and-step footwork here, as it helps you to cover distance easily.

a)

b)

THE ELUSIVE OPPONENT

Against a fast, elusive fighter who bobs and weaves and is hard to hit, you have to realise that if his body is moving fast and is slippery, his legs won't normally move particularly well. Fighters either move the legs or the upper body. First, move in and trap his legs by stepping through his stance or trapping his foot. Hit him as he adjusts his base. Second, kick to the legs to make him move his legs. His upper body will slow down while he is moving, so attack the upper body till

he slips and bobs again. Then go back to attacking the base. Alternatively, make sure that you mix the lines that you attack on. Deliver a number of direct strikes; then switch to strike up and down the centre line. Finally, use left and right hooks at the mid-section. He won't know which way to evade if you keep your strikes seemingly coming from all angles.

12.5 > A FAST, ELUSIVE OPPONENT, a-b) unable to get a good shot, c-f) attack opponent's base by stepping across his leg.

a)

b)

c)

d)

e)

f)

THE HARD HITTER

The hard hitter is a real problem. He could be heavier or simply have better mechanics than you. Your strategy here has to be to spike his guns, so to speak, by crushing all of his blows. When he gets more circumspect in throwing punches, enter in close, and unleash a flurry of blows, before quickly moving away. Remember to avoid going backwards in a straight line. If you're in close, then you're at the centre of a circle. To exit, rotate slightly and go out on a different angle than the one you came in on.

12.6 > CRUSHING ALL BLOWS, a-b) use elbow crushes to discourage the hard hitter, c) similarly you can crush a hard kicker.

a)   b)   c)

THE GOOD KICKER

The main problem with good kickers is that, whatever kick you block, there's either a hand attack coming as a follow up, or the first kick was a fake and you're walking into his next attack. Trust me, I've done this a few times and a big shin bone across your face isn't particularly nice. Your first strategy is to close most of the lines, leaving just one open. Then, attach or jam the kick when it comes, where you've given it the opening.

Alternatively, draw him until he starts to attack deeper, then stand your ground and stop hit or let his kick slip by you and counter hit. Mentally make the decision that you will only go forwards, regardless of what he does, and you'll be too near for his kick to have destructive power. Also, hopping in behind a raised knee with a good guard will mean that his major tool is compromised and you're on more of an even playing field.

12.6 > COUNTERING A GOOD KICKER, a) overhook and attack his standing leg, b) hop in behind a raised knee with a good guard, c) stop hit his standing leg.

a)   b)   c)

THE GOOD PUNCHER

Good hand skills are hard to defend against, but there are a couple of ways to deny him his strongest card. Basic front kicks work really well against those not well-versed in kicking. If your kicks connect, his hands will come down and you can often prevail, as long as you're not there for too long. The other option is to use the long knee. For him to punch well to your head, he has to expose his ribs. Knee away and grab-and-knee if he's really near, so that you deny him his range. Use of the long guard is invaluable here as it keeps him at a distance where you can kick his legs, or, even better, long-knee him. Realise that circular techniques are easier for a committed fighter to come in on, whereas direct thrusting techniques spike him and keep him away. Practise using your kicks when your distance is being closed down.

THE GRAPPLER

Grapplers seem to come in two flavours: those who know how to strike, and those that don't. They're both dangerous, but the ones who haven't been hit before often turn their heads away, and you can strike at will. However, be careful and don't be too greedy. Even a light attachment on your sleeve could find you flying through the air if your opponent has good throwing skills. Don't go in to close range, but keep him on the end of fast, snappy blows with good retraction. Often they are susceptible to fakes, once you've hit them once or twice.

Against the grappler who knows about striking, you have to realise that it's easier to 'know' about striking and grappling, but hard to be good in both areas. Keep him at distance, as above, and strike as he tackles, then keep hitting if you end up on the ground. Don't play his game, but strike and get up if possible. Research basic groundwork so you know the game, but realise that most grapplers will be stronger than you. It's less likely that they'll be accomplished strikers. Think out of the box. Why are you trying to grapple with a grappler? Do what you do best and attack his weak points.

THE TRAPPER

Against the trapper, or someone who wants to attach, the thing is to realise early on what their strategy is. I remember sparring with a senior student of mine who was also an experience Wing Chun stylist. Overall, I was a better fighter than him, but I tried to attach and got hit a number of times, and I could feel the control of the fight ebbing away from me. I'd gone into his area. To counter this, I pulled my limbs in closer, made my attacks snappier, and refused to be manipulated. Then I used body evasion and angling to deliver a variety of curved and straight hits, and bingo, I was doing much better. This taught me that you have to assess people early and don't stray where they are strong. Whilst body manipulation and trapping can help your game, they can also be your downfall if that's your opponent's strength. Don't try to out-trap a specialist.

CHAPTER 13 Mind

Controlling your own thoughts whilst keeping his under attack is what you need to do here. Master fighters don't only beat you physically but have often won with a look before the start. Working on your own thoughts and fears and staying positive whilst making your opponent doubt his own abilities and frustrate his intentions is something you can study even when away from the dojo or ring. This is one of the most infinite areas for you to work on and impacts all areas of your life.

Controlling your opponent

The more you can control the actions of your opponent, or frustrate him, the better. Your aim is to be a puppet master and to take control of the situation. In some instances, play with the speed, timing and frequencies that he works on. In others, make it painful for him to attack, with the aim of seeing the resultant frustration (or pain) on his face. You need to diminish his abilities, make him doubt his skills and frustrate his plans. Above all you need to feel in control.

MORSE CODE

Let's start with what I call the 'Morse code' drill. Keep an extended jab in his face. It doesn't have to hit hard, it's just there, in his face. Pulse it like Morse code. When he parries, just put your hand back as soon as possible. When he goes to hit you hard, fade back out of distance and then as soon as possible come back to applying the Morse code. Because it's soft and fluid, it can flow around blocks or parries. Your only aim is to keep it in his face. Important: you have to have a long stance and be able to snap back or use footwork to get out of range. Think of it like Muhammad Ali's fighting style and you've got the idea. This can be incredibly frustrating for a fighter to have done against them as it says that you don't respect their skills, and from your part it's a fairly low risk strategy. A frustrated fighter doesn't operate well; he's stiff, angry and unfocussed.

CRUSH EVERYTHING

This is a simple concept that again attacks his core self-belief whilst being fairly low risk for you. Like all these things, don't do it all the time. Just do it enough to make him start to think that he's inept and then reap the benefits. In this instance you crush all of his blows, both hands and legs. Think of yourself as a rocky outcrop on which he's going to founder. Keep a dispassionate look in your eye, and don't show any pain if you do get hurt. Keep it simple, with vertical and rear diagonal crushes for the hands, and a bias for a single leg for the leg crushes. If your skills are more developed, you can use both legs. It just has to work, and look easy.

WIND UP AND LET DOWN

Humans copy or mimic one another's behaviour to fit into social units such as their families or tribes. This is hard-wired into us; you'll see people copying each other frequently in sparring. One person throws a jab, and the other does the same thing. It's either innate or they've got no imagination. Set a fast tempo and wait for him to join in. Then when he's locked in to this tempo, drop him by stopping what you're doing and walk away to distance and do nothing. Alternatively change the tempo markedly to a much slower one. They normally realise they've been wound up and relax too much, or join in the lower tempo with you, and then you hit them hard and fast. Think of it as winding them up and letting them down. It's easier to get them to join when the tempo starts at a fast pace.

> **TIP:**
>
> Often, beginners, and even experienced fighters, show what they feel on their faces, letting their opponent know about their internal psychological landscape. Show nothing or have a gentle smile. Be like a cold-hearted hunter. If you get hit, don't moan at yourself, or tut, or titter – this just lets them know they are getting to you. They are as unsure as you and looking for feedback on their success. Don't give it to them.

DIFFERING SPEEDS

Here you prey on his need to focus on the frequencies that could be harmful to him. Much like a radio scanner, his brain works best when focused on a small range of speeds. Start out fast as he'll respond better to fast movement. Nothing really has to hit (although it can) – it just has to threaten. The aim is to make him think, 'right, I have to concentrate here'. What will happen is that his brain will start to focus only on things that are happening at the fast end of the frequency range. Once he's there, walk in slowly with no show of intent and bash him cleanly, then walk out again. Sometimes it can be a slow punch or, more rarely, a kick. Because it's not at the threatening end of the frequency range it sometimes seems like you are invisible. I've had really high-level fighters say, 'I never saw you'.

Even if this doesn't work for you, the basic strategy of playing with his tempo gives you a great sense of control (even if it's illusory!). You become a more relaxed fighter. He, in return, gets a general feeling of not being in control. Play all of these tempo games together and you've got a potent strategy. As a fighter, you need to engage and disengage. Think all the time about changing the rhythm, about imposing your presence and then disappearing. Think about controlling space. Be there and then not there. Finally, change how you feel to them; sometimes strong, then soft and yielding, or quick and stinging. Don't use these things too much: alternate one or two per week while you practise.

'Float like a butterfly, sting like a bee'
DREW BUNDINI BROWN / MUHAMMAD ALI

HAVING IT DONE TO YOU

If your on the receiving end of the tempo games, realise that the copying / partnering dynamic works both ways, even though he initiated it. This time, instead of him dropping you or walking in slowly, you do it to him. You are equally in control.

GETTING HIT

What happens when you get hit? Nobody likes to get hit. When I was young and worked with lots of boxers I'd often hear them saying things like 'he hasn't got much of a punch', after a fight. As someone who didn't know anything about fighting, I thought 'surely any punch must hurt'. However, once you've been punched with a gloved hand a few times, you realise that there is a whole range of quality in strikes. Some are light, others are clubbing and a few are truly frightening. I don't advocate getting hit if you can help it, but you shouldn't allow yourself to be uptight or nervous about getting hit in sparring. Remember that 'talk test' stuff at the beginning. What we're building is skill and experience, so you shouldn't be getting hit too hard anyway.

In truth your imagination is the worst thing. Very few punches are as painful as they might be in your imagination, or at least the pain is usually short-lived. If you work on keeping your game tight, and also expect to get hit occasionally, then you'll do much better in sparring. Lots of people think that because they've done some training, they won't get hit. This only happens to fictional secret agent characters or movie martial arts masters. The truth is that everyone gets hit to some extent. Once you accept that you'll get hit then, incredibly, you become much harder to hit. Don't overreact to fakes: this will take you off-line and leave your centre line open to be attacked. Rather, build up your tolerance to contact by practicing the head-hitting drill we did before and work on your defence. Then you'll realise that very few clean shots get through and clean shots are the ones that hurt. Remember that your imagination is your greatest enemy. Just deal with the reality of what actually happened and you'll do really well. The human body is very durable – yes, including yours. Be sensible in your training and you'll get tougher without getting hurt.

CHAPTER 14 Conclusion

Sparring isn't easy but during the study of it you'll learn lots about yourself. In the process you'll build self-discipline, courage, and determination and, surprisingly, love and respect for your opponents and training partners.

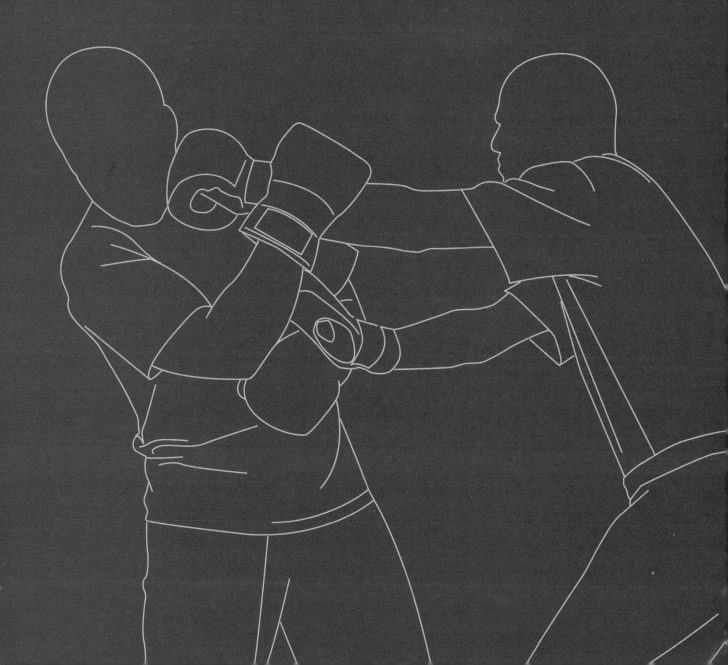

If you've followed this book all the way through then you should now be sparring fairly regularly and building and effective toolbox of technique. To continue making progress you need to set defined and achievable goals that you can work towards. This can be quite hard to do in sparring. How do you define the indefinable? My advice would be to focus on your peers, people in your school who you want to be able to hold your own with, or be able to dominate, and set a target date for specific achievements to motivate yourself. You may not achieve everything but it will give you focus. Sparring is a percentages game so work on improving your percentages, first in defence, then in attack or counter attack.

It's essential that you set objectives that are possible to achieve so that you can mark your success and ultimate aims that will challenge you to the extreme. Always make sure that you are achieving success and that sparring and training are fundamentally positive experiences. The occasional set back can then be put in its rightful place. Re-evaluate and re-assess your objectives often – maybe your step towards your ultimate goal was too big? Think positively at all times and only train with those who are similarly of a positive nature.

In all areas of your training don't become obsessed by simply adding new techniques. You want to develop the ability to see themes, shapes and positions and to anchor techniques to these stable centres. Research your own experience but keep your answers simple so you'll be more successful more often. Don't let your work ethic get the better of you. Some people don't want to win as much as to work hard and get the fix that exercise gives – or maybe they just like getting hit! The aim is to make opponents work hard and for you to do the minimum necessary. Don't make it more complicated than it is.

Realise that it's going to take a long time and you have to be patient. Some concepts you can't understand unless you've got a couple of years under your belt. One of my senior students who had lots of previous martial arts experience said that he only really understood things I'd been telling him when he'd been training with me for some five years. Aim to achieve that rare mix of toughness and cleverness where you don't need to get hit to show how tough you are, but can take a hit when it comes. There are lots of tough guys around but tough clever guys are a rare breed. Be patient and enjoy the trip.

Technically, make sure you work your basics often and in as many variations as possible. There's nothing like doing repetitions but you also need to see the big picture, of where, and when to use a technique. Most importantly, practise your techniques in sparring. Actively engage your

mind with these techniques and focus on one at a time. Get your single techniques to work first and then work on combinations. At any one time, hold a self-image of yourself as a specialist, be it a thrower, kicker, knockout puncher etc., then you'll be more successful.

Keep things tight with a good guard so that there's less room for him to get his strikes in. This is essential. Try not to implement defensive techniques one at a time, reactively. You should have them happening all the time in a minimized way.

The timing aspect of certain techniques can be hard to learn. Realise that timing and distance are the big things and study these in depth. Watch great fighters and see how they use the same moves. Don't get caught up in the fight itself, but look for the different attributes that are on show. Try to emulate the feel in your own training.

Remember active mistakes are better than passive ones. Competition is great, it's not real fighting but it's a great way of testing yourself and a great way of gaining confidence. What type of competition is the best? Whichever is your preference is the answer. You're up against strangers and they don't know about your reputation, or training, or lack thereof. Competition hones your ability to deal with fear. This is one of the big things to gain control over. Stepping up to the line or stepping in the ring takes real courage, whatever the level. So go ahead and stretch yourself. 'Pain lasts a moment, but glory lasts forever' as the quote goes.

If you find yourself afraid during training then don't doggedly persevere at the same level or you will become completely gun shy. Go back a level, drill and spar at an easy level so you get your confidence back. Everyone's been scared at one time or other. I had a two year period where I was scared stiff all the time, but paradoxically, fighting really well. Above all be kind to yourself and give yourself permission to not have to be a super hero everyday. Take your time, do the work and spar with mentors and friends who will go at the pace you need to get back up to the level you want. Remember this should be fun and overall a joyful and exhilarating experience.

Rotate your skill focus periodically and realise that you can always be tighter, faster, more supple. Consistency and attention to weak spots is the secret in all your training and will get you where you want to go. Use video and other modern aids to help you turbo charge your progress Above all, aim high, train with the best and you'll become the best. Where possible fight the best, you'll get hurt less than fighting someone of lesser skill. It takes time, patience and intelligent practice to become great at sparring.

Enjoy the trip.

Acknowledgement

I wrote this book as I realised that there weren't any books out there on sparring. Very few books seem to have the student in mind, to provide answers to those questions that come up every day. I know from my teaching experience that sparring is a constant cause of concern for students. This book should go part of the way to explaining some of the variations and possibilities available to you. It's been hard to put down in print what is a very fluid and dynamic form. I hope you think it's been worth the effort.

This book wouldn't have been possible without the help of an incredible team of people. First, Stephanie de Howes laid the book out and did all the graphic design. She spent countless hours working over my sometimes jumbled text and turning it into something better. Thanks also to Jamie Hutchins who edited the book a number of times and made many suggestions that improved the end result for the reader both grammatically and in terms of layout.

On the photographic front, I had a great team of instructors to act as models. I couldn't have shown the techniques any better - any mistakes apparent are because I chose the wrong pictures. This is a group of incredible instructors and it was a great pleasure to get them together all at the same time. My sincere thanks to Dave Birkett, Neil McLeod, Wayne Rowlands, Owen Ogbourne, Steve Wright, Steve Martin, Carl Jackson, Paul Hill, Steve Payne Kim VanDoren and of course the wonderful Judy Breen.

Finally, it's normally hard to find a photographer who really understands how to take martial arts photographs. I was overjoyed that I was able to get Pete Drinkell to do this book. Pete took all the photos for my previous book, *Fighting - a path to understanding*, and he's always a joy to work with.

I hope you enjoy the book and that it helps you on your path. If you want to continue your training online or in person, check out our website, www.bobbreen.com.

Good training.

Bob Breen

Resources

Books

The Art of War
Sun Tzu, translated by Thomas Cleary (1998).
Shambhala Publications Inc.

Boxing Finess: A Guide to Get Fighting Fit
Ian Oliver (2005). London: Snowbooks.

Fighting
Bob Breen (2006). London: Snowbooks.

**The 7 Habits of Highly Effective People:
Powerful Lessons in Personal Change**
Stephen R. Covey (2004), 15th Anniversary Ed.
The Free Press

Tao Te Ching
Lao Tzu (1990), Shambhala Publications Inc;
New Ed edition.

Tao of Jeet Kune Do
Bruce Lee (1975), Ohara Publications Inc.,U.S.

**Training for Warriors:
The Ultimate Mixed Martial Arts Workout**
Martin Rooney (2008), HarperCollins Publishers.

DVDs

Panantukan 1 & 2
Panantukan or Filipino Boxing is like English Boxing with all the dirty tricks left in. Striking, unbalancing, limb destructions, arm breaking and wrenches are just some of the skills demonstrated on these DVDs. The second DVD adds unique sweeping, tripping and throwing techniques which truly make this and incredible art for self-defence. With Panantukan you control your opponent before they attempt to strike – essential to take your empty hand skills to the highest level

Single Stick 1-3
These DVDs use a step by step approach showing you how to make the fundamentals really work. DVD 1 concentrates on long range attack and defence; DVD 2 covers the medium range, showing blocks, counter for counter, and practice drills, concentrating on details of position and footwork; DVD 3 covers drills such as Sombrada, Abecedario and transitions between ranges. The emphasis is on simplicity and realism, which is typical of Bob's functional approach.

Knife Defence
The Filipino Martial Arts have one of the most effective approaches to knife defence and Bob is one of the leading experts in the field. On this DVD he demonstrates how to control, disarm and take away the knife from an attacker. Defences work against simple single attacks but also against more realistic multiple thrusts and slashes.

Sword and Dagger
Sword and Dagger or 'Espada y Daga' is one of the key elements of the Filipino Martial Art of Kali. Equally applied to any long and short weapons (e.g. stick and knife) or empty hands fighting, this is viewed by many as the highest form of the art and the key to understanding the structure of combat more effectively.

www.bobbreen.com